1989

WOMEN WAR CORRESPONDENTS OF WORLD WAR II

WOMEN WAR
CORRESPONDENTS
OF WORLD WAR II

Lilya Wagner

Contributions in Women's Studies, Number 104

GREENWOOD PRESS

NEW YORK
WESTPORT, CONNECTICUT
LONDON

Library of Congress Cataloging-in-Publication Data

Wagner, Lilya.
    Women war correspondents of World War II / Lilya Wagner.
        p. cm.—(Contributions in women's studies, ISSN 0147-104X ;
  no. 104)
    Includes index.
    Bibliography: p.
    ISBN 0–313–26287–X (lib. bdg. : alk. paper)
    1. War correspondents—United States—Biography. 2. World War,
  1939–1945—Journalists—Biography. 3. World War, 1939–1945—Women—
  Biography. I. Title. II. Series.
  D799.U6W34 1989
  940.53'15'042—dc19   89–1981

British Library Cataloguing in Publication Data is available.

Library of Congress Catalog Card Number: 89–1981
ISBN: 0–313–26287–X
ISSN: 0147–104X

First published in 1989

Greenwood Press, Inc.
88 Post Road West, Westport, Connecticut 06881

Printed in the United States of America

The paper used in this book complies with the
Permanent Paper Standard issued by the National
Information Standards Organization (Z39.48–1984).

10 9 8 7 6 5 4 3 2 1

Copyright Acknowledgments

The author and publisher gratefully acknowledge permission to use the following:

"Frau Himmler Maintains She is Still Proud of Her Husband," "Torgau Meeting With Russians is Both Gay and Strenuous," "Mrs. Mussolini Weepingly Recalls Her Happy Early Days with Dead Dictator," "Yanks Dash Ahead in Race for Rhine" by Ann Stringer are reprinted courtesy of United Press International.

"Globe Writer Recalls 'Her Greatest Thrill,' " by Iris Carpenter and quotations from various letters to the editor are reprinted courtesy of The Boston Globe.

"Japs Can't Beat Goin' Jesse, John D., Curly" by Bonnie Wiley and various Associated Press dispatches by Ruth Cowan are reprinted courtesy of The Associated Press.

"Gen. Clark Strong in Praise of Hawaii Troops of 422nd" by Lyn Crost is reprinted courtesy of the Honolulu Star-Bulletin.

"Americans and Russians Join Forces at the Elbe" by Catherine Coyne is reprinted with permission of the Boston Herald.

"Autobiographical sketch by Sigrid Schultz" is reprinted courtesy of the Tribune Company.

Excerpts from *The Face of War*. Copyright © 1988 by Martha Gellhorn. Reproduced here by permission of the Atlantic Monthly Press.

Special thanks to Lyn Crost, Tania Long Daniell, Catherine Coyne Hudson, Flora Lewis, Shelley Mydans, Helen Thomas, and Bonnie Wiley for the use of quotations from various letters.

Dedicated to
my brother, Velyo Vinglas,
who had a profound and positive influence
on my personal and professional development—
who encouraged me, loved me, and accepted me—
With much love and appreciation

Contents

Acknowledgments

The very idea of locating women who had reported from the scenes of World War II seemed impossible. Little about these women was recorded in the literature on journalism. A few names surfaced during a preliminary search, but not with much accompanying information.

Most journalists, when approached with the idea, were enthusiastic, but could offer little help beyond encouragement. A few, however, saw the possibilities and supplied help at the start of this research as well as during its progress.

Ruth Holmberg, publisher of the *Chattanooga Times* and a member of the family that established the *New York Times,* was the first to provide assistance that would eventually lead to a long trail of research much like the uncovering of a mystery. She provided names of possible subjects as well as names of journalists who could give more information.

From the first beginnings of this search process a name surfaced frequently—that of Barney Oldfield. A graduate of the University of Nebraska/Lincoln School of Journalism prior to World War II, he served with the U.S. Army in Europe and knew much of the activities of the reporters as well as the reporters themselves. He provided a great deal of helpful background information and never stopped giving useful hints as the search progressed.

Always helpful and encouraging were Dr. Wilma Crumley and Dr. Larry Walklin from the University of Nebraska/Lincoln School of Journalism.

To discover just the names of the reporters was not an easy task; much more difficult was to learn the whereabouts of the individuals. Many professionals in the field of journalism assisted in the laborious process and made it interesting and fascinating all the while.

The subjects themselves, with very few exceptions, are to be thanked for their almost unanimous support and interest. Their cooperation and encouragement is much appreciated.

Finally, the help of Shawn Patrick Nowlan, Jennifer Schmitt, John Wagner, Linda Skinner, and Laurence Downing, during the final stages of manuscript preparation was most valuable and appreciated.

WOMEN WAR CORRESPONDENTS OF WORLD WAR II

Introduction

Although the history of journalism contains names of women who made a significant impact on the field—from the colonial widow printer, the big city reporter, the sob sister, the war correspondent, to the postwar pioneers—the literature that discusses the accomplishments of women in journalism is scarce and limited. Yet just a brief acquaintance with details about any one of these women would indicate that women journalists have always been a potent force in the field, although largely ignored in a listing of accomplishments.

Some attempts have been made to document the significant contributions of women to the field of journalism. While these are credible as well as interesting, they merely touch on the highlights of women's experience in journalism. One segment of women's history of journalism that lends itself to serious study involves war correspondents.

When World War II began, most American newsmen wanted to get to the front, where the "big story" was. They faced problems correspondents had not been troubled with in previous wars—increased censorship, the war being fought on several different fronts, and the dangers of then modern warfare. Journalists, however, managed to carry out their responsibilities in a commendable manner. Shortly after the war ended, Secretary of War Robert P. Patterson said at a dinner honoring war correspondents:

World War II was the most thoroughly reported war in history. . . . When we consider the scale of the struggle, the speed of operations, the great distances covered and the startling scientific developments, the very quantity of the coverage is a credit to the press . . . and to the men and women who made that coverage possible. It was in the quality of reporting, however, that the coverage

of World War II reached the high peak. The reporters and photographers were
honest, competent, and patriotic. The few exceptions served to accentuate the
merits of the vast majority.[1]

Communications media were aware that the demand for news was
great, and correspondents, including women, were eager to go to the
scenes of action. Women, however, sometimes had to take a circuitous
route to get to the big story. As Flora Lewis stated, "It was easier for
a newcomer [woman] to get a reporting job once the U.S. entered the
war and the men went off."[2] Sometimes this was the entry point for a
woman who eventually joined the ranks of men reporters in the war
theater. Marion Marzolf reports that World War II left vacancies on
the newspapers, and women entered the field to do a variety of jobs:
serve as copy editors, set type and run presses, and in a few cases,
become foreign correspondents. "By 1943 women made up 50 percent
of the staffs of many newspapers in small cities and this trend was
expected to continue."[3] Women began to cover nearly everything, in
large cities as well as foreign areas.

Marzolf states that "the war brought them to the front zone and they
roughed it as bravely as any soldier and turned in their share of
scoops."[4] Their accomplishments, however, weren't easily won. The
State Department issued passports and the War Department accredited correspondents, but neither department was eager to extend
rights or consideration to women reporters. It took everything from
diplomacy to subterfuge to win the coveted accreditation and passport.

Colonel Barney Oldfield served as a public relations officer during
World War II and was assigned the duty of establishing press camps—
something that had no precedent. Each press camp was to be a facility
attached to the regular military forces, capable of handling administration, transportation, communication, and briefings, and each was to
follow a field army across Western Europe. There would be fifty
correspondents in each of these camps. First the correspondent would
be accredited to his or her country, then join a press camp and follow
the army's activities as closely as was safe.

From this vantage point Oldfield was to observe many war correspondents who came and went through the three press camps he
established for the First, Third and Ninth Armies. He had to contend
with all kinds, from those who persisted in putting their lives in danger,
to those who liked to stay put in the press camp and write from the
briefings rather than forage for stories. "So the press camp became a
capsule of extraordinary life along the front," he recalled in an inter-

view. There was gung-ho competition, much character assassination, and something that was a tremendous annoyance, the "magic carpet" correspondent, one who would put down a dateline even though he'd never been there. "It was like being housemother to a nest of snakes in many cases," Oldfield states.

War correspondents, according to General Eisenhower, were to be treated as quasi staff officers, and he wanted them to carry the rank of captain, as designated in the terms of the Geneva Convention. Eisenhower saw the press as a conduit to public opinion in the United States, and felt everything should be done to make it possible for them, within the limits of military security, to perform their journalistic function. The rank of captain allowed correspondents, in the event of being captured, the protective privileges provided by the Geneva Convention.

Oldfield was one of the earliest supporters of the rights of women war correspondents. He felt that "if they wanted to take those risks, and if getting the story meant that much to them, if their future professional status was worth these kinds of risks, why should we stand in the way?" Oldfield realized that war correspondents wanted to be in Europe and the Mediterranean not only to get the big story, but also because they saw this as a way to a big future. A reputation as a war correspondent would pave the way for career advancement, many reporters felt, and this did become true (particularly evident when one studies the complete roster of accredited war correspondents and finds names such as John Steinbeck and Walter Cronkite). Oldfield did not feel it was fair to deny women these privileges.

Regulations for women varied, and sometimes there was a stipulation in effect that prevented women war correspondents from going any farther than the women's services were allowed. At times this could be a handicap, at other times a bonanza. Oldfield explains: "If the battalion aid medical teams included a nurse or more, the women correspondents could get as close to the front as the battalion headquarters, and that was as close as you needed to get unless you wanted to be captured." However, the women met with a variety of obstacles, in spite of the open-mindedness of officers like Oldfield. He recalls that "women . . . continued all through the war to be the subject of a great debate. Every time allocations for spaces came up, someone was bound to suggest that the women stay with field-hospital units where nurses were already provided for or not go at all."[5] This type of mentality caused great difficulties for the women professionals. They faced antagonism from generals such as Montgomery, who had no use for women on the war scene, and from men reporters who either held deep biases against the opposite sex or who were simply fearful of competition from a new front.

Yet the women persisted, and the subjects of this book each had accounts to relate that held similarities as well as differences. But they were there, and did a commendable job of reporting. M.L. Stein quoted correspondent H.R. Knickerbocker who said, "Whenever you find hundreds of thousands of sane people trying to get out of a place and a little bunch of madmen struggling to get in—you know the latter are newspapermen."6 Presumably Stein meant "newspapermen" in terms of "humankind" because the women struggled to get to the big story, and while there encountered challenges and opportunities they had not always expected.

Women reporters may have had disadvantages as war correspondents, but, as Colonel Oldfield put it during an interview, "When the story got back to wherever was its ultimate destination, the reporters were judged on the journalistic merits of the story—not whether or not it was produced by a woman."

One of the subjects of this book, Lyn Crost, stated that "we should not be portrayed as heroines. We were where we wanted to be, doing what we wanted to do. The same is true of men who were war correspondents."7 Being at the scene of the big story because they wanted to appears to be the main intent of virtually all the subjects (except for a few whose main reason for going appeared to be to accompany their husbands). Consequently, these women did not expect and, indeed, did not want any preferential treatment and did all they could to avoid exceptional notice. Crost added that "there are good and poor men reporters as well as good and poor women reporters, not only in wartime coverage but also in everyday domestic coverage."8 Granted, women reporters were fewer in number and therefore more noticeable, particularly in an ambience that was almost exclusively male-dominated. Women reporters, according to their own accounts, did encounter problems unique to their sex, but in general were adept at handling these problems and did their jobs as professionally as would be required of any journalist anywhere.

As the women who are discussed in the next chapters were located, they were asked questions about their experiences, including the conditions under which they reported, the types of stories they wrote, and their accomplishments as journalists. The women who are featured in this book were largely newspaper or wire-service reporters who reported from the front. A few other reporters who wrote for magazines were included because of particularly interesting experiences or personalities. Excluded from this study were broadcast journalists, most magazine writers, and commentators. Some women received ninety-day passes to the war front, and then wrote upon their return to their home base in the United States. These were excluded as well.

During World War II, these women journalists worked in a career and geographic area of reporting still dominated by men. The generalizations that can be made about the women journalists who were interviewed are few. One assumption—that women reporters had a difficult time because of male biases against them—was not valid in every case. Some women felt these biases hampered them, some found them a mere annoyance, some didn't sense any at all, and in a few cases claims were made that men actually enhanced the women's careers.

One general conclusion about the experiences of these women is that they reported from the war scene because that's where the big story was. Almost without exception (except where the primary role was of wife and then reporter) the women wanted to be part of a dramatic and exhilarating scene as much as the journalists who happened to be men.

Also almost without exception the women included in this book were unique, for differing reasons. Some showed exceptional courage, others exceptional perception in terms of material reported. Others were, simply stated, "characters" who are memorable because of their personalities.

The subjects of this book reflected statements made by Marzolf, who commented that war did not necessarily create a newspaperwoman but gave her greater opportunities in the journalism field. When the war ended, some women hired to fill in during an emergency left their positions, some were released against their will, some married and had families. Some women, especially those who filled in during an emergency, weren't exceptional and knew it, and therefore left journalism. Others, however, were good. They were professionals who had an opportunity to excel in the field, and these were not edged out by men returning from reporting the war. As Genevieve P. Herrick of the *Chicago Tribune* said (quoted in Marzolf), "Inez Robb in North Africa and Ruth Cowan of the AP were both doing unusual jobs, but they did good work in peacetime as well as wartime. The unusual woman is likely always to have unusual assignments, and the woman journalist was making the most of her wartime opportunities."9

NOTES

All material in quotation marks throughout the book that is not credited to a source by an endnote is from personal interviews with the subjects of the particular chapters. Clippings used as resource material sometimes lacked full bibliographic information. These were supplied by the subjects of this book and the original sources were not available.

1. "Task of Occupation Declared in Peril," *New York Times* 23 November 194?

2. Flora Lewis, letter to author, 18 February 1985.

3. Marion Marzolf, *Up from the Footnote* (New York: Hastings House, 1977), 69.

4. Ibid.

5. Barney Oldfield, *Never a Shot in Anger* (New York: Duell, Sloan and Pearce, 1956), 53.

6. M.L. Stein, *Under Fire: The Story of American War Correspondents* (New York: Julian Messner, 1968), 228.

7. Lyn Crost, letter to author, 19 September 1986.

8. Ibid.

9. Marzolf, *Up from the Footnote*, 72.

1

Ann Stringer

When Prime Minister Groza of Rumania was interviewed during the World War II period, he asked wistfully of every American correspondent, "When is Ann Stringer of the United Press coming back? She had the most beautiful legs in Rumania."[1]

This same war correspondent was fond of saying, "I'm a newspaperman. I'm not a newspaperwoman. I can write the pants off of any man."[2] And she did–she was the first reporter to meet Russian soldiers at Torgau and not only witness but write about an important slice of the war's history, and the first one to report on the exciting linkup between U.S. and Russian forces.

Ann Stringer was born on December 9, 1918, in Eastland, Texas. Her parents, Tom and Bernie Harrell, were both college-educated and teachers, and Ann inherited their love for knowledge. She graduated from the University of Texas with degrees in journalism and English. While on the Austin campus she met Bill Stringer and they were married in San Antonio in 1941.

Bill joined United Press in Dallas, and then the couple was transferred to Columbus, Ohio. Ann found various jobs until the *Columbus Citizen* took her on. Finally, UP offered her a job, yet she hesitated. She wasn't sure it was wise to have a husband-wife team, since it could be difficult for his career. But friends convinced her otherwise. Then they were transferred to Argentina, South America. They reported from the various South American capitals on stories such as the revolution in Argentina when Peron grasped power.

They were happy both personally and professionally—except for a desire to write about the big story happening in Europe. That's where they both wanted to be. They returned to New York, and when a transfer didn't come, Bill accepted an offer from Reuters, a British news agency. Ann stayed with UP, but decided that as soon as she received her accreditation as a war correspondent she would also join Reuters. In the meantime, Bill went to Europe. Ann waited impatiently until the time she could meet him and once again they would work as a team.

In June of 1944 Ann showed up for work at Reuters. The manager of the news agency engaged her in small talk and asked questions such as, "What are your plans after the war?" Ann became a bit impatient; she was anxious to get to work. The next Thursday she would be shipped to the war theater in Europe. While they were talking she was called to the phone. She heard a colleague from London say, "I hope this isn't true." Ann answered, "You've known all along that I was going to join Reuters." Then he told her, "Bill has been killed."

Bill and two others were trying to make it to Paris before the Allied armies when a German tank spotted them and fired point-blank into the jeep. Bill was killed on D-Day.

Ann canceled her sailing date because "I had to think things through. It didn't take long to realize that the only thing to do was go on and do what we had planned to do together." UP invited her to return and she sailed to Europe as a war correspondent.

First she went to London. Bill Higginbotham of UP in London horrified the whole shop when he put her in charge of the news desk. "That was interesting, but it wasn't the front, which was where I wanted to be," she says. She toured air force bases, and during her first weekend Lady Astor called her for an interview. And when Lady Astor resigned from Parliament, she again called Ann for an interview. Unfortunately, Ann had already gone to the continent. Lady Astor chose to give UP the interview anyway, because she had liked Ann.

Ann was an "honest beauty," as others described her. With dark hair tumbling past her shoulders, a full mouth, and pale blue, heavily lidded eyes, she had a sophisticated yet direct and innocent face. Barney Oldfield referred to her as "Ann, with her butter-melting eyes." "Ann Stringer never moved across the rear areas without causing something of a sensation," Oldfield relates. Once she was riding in a jeep, her long hair flowing behind her, when there came the familiar whistles. " 'You'd think,' said Hank [Wales, a *Chicago Tribune* reporter] . . . 'them guys never saw a jeep before.' "3

But this "beauty queen," one of three reporters dubbed the "Rhine Maidens" (the other two were Iris Carpenter and Lee Carson), produced some of the finest reporting of the war. As a male colleague put it, "When she got her chance she made it brilliantly good."4

Ann then went on to Paris and finally to Maastricht, Holland, on the Belgian frontier. There she was ordered by the Supreme Headquarters Allied European Forces (SHAEF) to return to Paris because women reporters were not to go beyond the point where female military personnel were allowed. Her first major headline had come from Juelich, a conquered German town. Barney Oldfield had the unpleasant task, back at the press camp, of telling her that her stay with the Ninth Army would be truncated if she continued to go further than permitted to the front lines. Juelich, of course, was off limits to Ann, and if Barney allowed the story to go through, he would also be in trouble. Hearing this edict, Ann burst into tears. But it was hard to deter Ann and she ignored this ultimatum, as she would many others. She didn't return to Paris but went forward. Neither did she send her stories by the wires but with various people who were going back and forth.

Ann earned quite a reputation, and people conjectured whether she was obsessed by Bill's death and therefore had a "death wish" herself. But Ann says, "I preferred to stay alive and get the story."

She went on to Remagen. The U.S. Army had captured the bridge, even though it was wired with explosives by the Germans. Her driver refused to cross the bridge, so she got out and walked across. Why? "Because that's where the big story was—on the other side of the Rhine," Ann states.

She filed her big story from Remagen, but again didn't send it over the press wires. "I just sent it out by messengers." She talked and listened to everyone involved with a story, and always followed up quickly and thoroughly, thereby continuing to build her reputation as an excellent war correspondent.

Then came the historic linkup of the American and Russian armies. Ann had heard rumors of the advancing Russians. She and a photographer, Allan Jackson of International News Service, arranged to fly in an L-5 Cub to try to spot the Russian army. They landed in a clover field on the west bank of the Elbe and walked toward a little village. She had to climb over two major road blocks. The village seemed deserted, but suddenly a young man came running down the street, his hair dripping wet. He wore nothing except shorts and a cap on his head with a red star on it. "That was my first Russian," Ann remembers.

The young soldier led them to the river bank where they found some battered racing shells. They rowed across, since all bridges had been demolished by the Germans. The Russians were celebrating by shooting their guns. They had gotten word that an American was there.

"Vive Truman, Vive Churchill, Vive Roosevelt," they shouted (they didn't know Roosevelt had died). Somehow the two Americans and the Russians made themselves understood to each other. "We were on the same emotional beam," Ann states.

Recalling this event in 1985, Ann wrote, "I had a great story, perhaps the greatest since the D-day landings, but it was worth nothing unless I could get it filed. . . . Also, I wasn't supposed to be there in the first place."5

Ann realized she would have to return to Paris quickly. She left the festivities at Torgau, crossed the Elbe in the small racing shell, and asked the pilot if he would fly her to Paris. He patiently explained he absolutely could not fly the L-5 to Paris, but he'd fly her as far west as possible. She took her typewriter and Allan Jackson's film and climbed in the plane. As they headed west, the pilot suddenly spotted a U.S. C-47 plane; it landed in a field and they landed beside it.

Ann rushed to the airmen and asked if they could take her to Paris. "What's the rush?" they inquired, somewhat amused and puzzled. She hurried to explain that she had just met the Russians and needed to get her story to Paris. They smiled knowingly and one replied, "Oh, yes. And I'm Stalin and he [his friend] is Roosevelt."

Ann didn't argue but settled under the wing of the plane and opened her typewriter. As she wrote, the airmen read over her shoulder. Suddenly it dawned on them—"She *did* meet the Russians! Let's go!" They headed for Paris and landed at the closest airfield. She then hitchhiked into Paris. At the Scribe Hotel, the press center for correspondents to the U.S. armies, she filed her story, her final frontline story. This story was the first to arrive in New York, reporting that the war was essentially over.

Then came her encounters with the concentration camps. She visited one that was not an extermination camp but a slave labor camp, where the inmates worked until they starved to death. In some of the bunks there was a dying person and a completely decomposed body on top of the person; the one below was too weak to crawl out. She and her companions saved the ones they could, got them out of the camp and into German homes where they had water and food, but it was almost hopeless. "It was unbelievable; you could stand there and watch and hear the groans and smell the stench, and you couldn't believe it." She went on to others—Buchenwald and Dachau. At Buchenwald she met the wife of the commandant, "the bitch of Buchenwald," who showed her the lampshades made of human skin. At Dachau the ovens were still smoking.

After the war ended, Ann covered the Nuremburg trials. On the morning they were to start, she went into the courthouse early, "just to sort of get the lay of the land inside," and there was a black G.I. arranging chairs and dusting, and singing in a beautiful voice, "Sometimes I Feel like a Motherless Child." He didn't know Ann was there, watching. "It had a sort of poetic meaning," Ann recalls, "just before the trials started."

The trials were not a pleasant thing; these were moving, anger-provoking days. Ann stayed until they were over, for approximately eleven months.

Ann kept up her reporting as she traveled through Europe, always in search of stories. She interviewed Pope Pius XII, then made headlines again a week later by interviewing Mussolini's widow. Another of her major stories was about the wife of Heinrich Himmler, whom she remembers as a cold and very detached woman who said that nobody likes a policeman, therefore her husband was not popular. She then went to Berlin, the divided city, and was one of the first reporters to find out what it was like in the Russian occupation zones. Finally, she visited Dresden, "a horror story." The American and British forces had made a thirty-six hour bombing raid and practically leveled it. The loss of art treasures because of the bombings horrified her. She felt that event was unnecessarily cruel, especially when she was told that more people were killed in that thirty-six hour raid than died at Hiroshima. That fact was neither verified nor proven untrue.

A highlight of her postwar reporting occurred in Vienna, at the press camp. She heard rumors in the mess hall that the great dancer Nijinsky was hiding in a cabin near Vienna. She got very excited and determined to locate him. She found him and his wife and spent pleasant times with them—and sometimes smuggled peanut butter sandwiches to them!

Ann's recollections of her experiences as a war correspondent include a commonsense attitude toward her position as a woman journalist. She didn't feel that the barriers were put up to keep her from getting the big stories, but to protect her. Her living conditions were spartan; she didn't have much money, and felt she didn't need any. Her pack of cigarettes in the K-rations was a form of money. "I was very popular on the way to the PX because I didn't smoke, and everybody wanted to escort me to the PX so they could have my ration!" One of the major handicaps for a woman was the facilities, and at the front there just weren't any. The women (and often she was the only one) could go to the generals' latrine but only under guard, and the guard remained stationed outside. "You nearly died before you admitted you had to go to the latrine! It was very embarrassing." Not long ago Ann received a letter from a correspondent who said she had given him one of the happiest days of his life. Ann was inside a latrine, and he was stationed outside when a general came up to enter it. Ann's guard said, "I'm sorry, you can't enter." The general turned to him and roared, "Have you lost every little bit of sense I thought you might have had?" The guard responded, "Well, general, if you do enter you'll be upbraided by a very irate woman correspondent." The general muttered, "Women, women!" but he waited until Ann, totally innocent about what was happening, emerged.

Ann had a difficult time returning to normalcy after the war ended because she couldn't shake Bill's memory. She tried to put her life together again. She married in 1948, but it didn't work. She married again in 1949 and the marriage lasted some thirty-five years, but these were not happy ones. She stuck with it, she says, because she had made a commitment. She devoted her time to helping her photographer husband, and let her own fine skills as a writer lie neglected. She divorced him in the early 1980s and took back her name, Ann Stringer.

Today Ann Stringer lives in New York and is gracious about sharing her memories and her friendship. She was a memorable and significant war correspondent, but even more memorable as a warm, responsive person.

On October 7, 1986, a tree was dedicated and a plaque unveiled at the Arlington National Cemetery to honor the more than two hundred war correspondents who were killed while reporting battles of the last hundred years. Among those honored was Bill Stringer. Ann wrote, "That October 7th had to be one of the most memorable days of my life."

SAMPLE OF WAR REPORTING BY ANN STRINGER

MRS. MUSSOLINI WEEPINGLY RECALLS HER HAPPY EARLY DAYS WITH DEAD DICTATOR

by Ann Stringer, United Press Staff Correspondent

A British Internment Camp, Terni, Italy, July 12. (UP) "I was never close to him when he was high: I was always near him when he was down."

With that weeping epitaph, Benito Mussolini's gray-haired widow summed up her life with the flamboyant Duce who left her for a younger, prettier mistress at the height of his Fascist power.

Pouring out her words between choking sobs, Donna Rachele revealed in an exclusive interview that she spoke to the doomed Duce by telephone only six hours before he was slain by a band of Italian partisans near Milan last April.

We spoke informally in the six-room apartment in an abandoned synthetic rubber factory where she and her two youngest children are being held in British protective custody.

Throughout the interview, Donna Rachele defended her dead husband against every accusation—except his final infidelity with Clara Petacci, who shared his death and humiliation in the bloody public square in Milan.

Hated Clara

For the red-haired Clara, Mrs. Mussolini had nothing but hatred and a fierce satisfaction that Benito's mistress was dead.

Her eyes literally flashed when Clara's name was mentioned. She pushed herself far back in her chair, sat up straight and spat out: "They've done well to hang her. She was the only one around Mussolini who had anything really to do with the Germans."

Then speaking even more furiously and pounding the table before her she almost shouted: "Mussolini (she always referred to him that way) never had anything to do with women. He never let them have any influence over him. That was propaganda just to ruin him."

She trembled with anger and emotion as she spoke, but the frail widow, still attractive in spite of her 50 years, maintained her dignity, presenting a far different picture from the hulking, peasant-type woman I have been led to expect. . . .

YANKS DASH AHEAD IN RACE FOR RHINE

United Press War Correspondent. Herreth, Germany, February 28 (UP)—It's a real breakthrough on the Rhineland front—Normandy is all over again!

Everything is moving, and moving fast.

The Yanks raced through this little town five and a half miles from Muenchen-Gladbach so fast they munched their K-rations on the march. They didn't even stop for a cup of water to wash them down.

German civilians had no time to seek shelter in their cellars as the war passed by them.

It's a razzle-dazzle race for the Rhine.

Prisoners are pouring in by the hundreds. Some told me they had marched 40 miles to reinforce the front line—only to find the Americans already were behind them.

All along the line, American command posts are on the move trying to catch up with their troops. Even the military police are not sure where the next post is located, what roads are safe or what towns are cleared.

One colonel said one of his battalions had been completely out of contact for the past 24 hours. Another had not been heard from since dawn.

Burning villages a few hundred yards off the line of march are bypassed without even a search. So long as there is no artillery fire from that direction, the doughboys keep going.

In many places, American and German medical men are tending wounded in the same shelters. They use the same ambulances and share medicine, bandages and stretchers. Some have been without sleep for 48 hours.

It's the kind of an advance generals dream about. But it's an advance in war. And in war, an advance is not just a game.

There is smoke, and piles of empty shells in ditches. There are ugly splotches of blood soaking into the mud.

There are scattered Nazi helmets hurled carelessly into fields beside the road. There are the rounder GI helmets, too.

And there is the unmistakable smell of an advance—heavy, hot and sweetish. It means that troops are moving so fast they haven't time to bury the enemy dead—or even their own sometimes.

Passing doughboys pause, perhaps to place a blanket, or maybe a bloodsoaked flag, over their own fallen comrades. But that's all they have time to do.

They have to keep marching, keep advancing. There's no stopping, no slowing down. They are headed for the Rhine.

And today the Rhine doesn't seem so far away.

TORGAU MEETING WITH RUSSIANS IS BOTH GAY AND STRENUOUS

By Ann Stringer, United Press War Correspondent. Sunday, April 29, 1945. Torgau, Germany, April 26 (Delayed)—Down the street of Torgau came a Russian youth wearing blue shorts and a gray cap with a red hammer and sickle on it.

"Bravo Americanski," he yelled. "Brave comrades."

He was dripping wet because he had swum the Elbe River to greet us. It was my first glimpse of the Russian Army.

I had just flown in a Piper Cub plane into this historic town where the official juncture of the Americans and Russians took place. We landed in a clover field, climbed over two road blocks and then saw the young Russian running up the street. A little earlier an American patrol had penetrated to Torgau.

The Elbe River is swarming with Russian soldiers, stripped to their shorts. They are swimming over to greet us. The Germans blew all the bridges across the Elbe, but there is a small fleet of shaky boats and canoes. I decided to cross the river in one of them and visit the Russians.

Soviets Greet Guests

As the Russians on the eastern bank saw us coming in our canoe they rushed down to the river bank through the tall, wet grass and began yelling greetings. They helped us drag the canoe up on the bank, and then they all stood rigidly at attention for a moment. One by one they stepped forward, saluted, shook hands and stepped back into line.

Then Lt. Grigori Otenchuku, a veteran of Stalingrad, stepped forward to make a formal speech in behalf of the Russians.

"A few months ago German soldiers were nearly in Stalingrad," he said. "Now Russian soldiers are in Berlin and Russian soldiers are here—all the way across Germany—with their American Allies."

Our party consisted of Lt. Myril Mayer of Wood River, Ill., and Lt. Raymond Worth of Galveston. The Russian soldiers insisted that we meet the commander of their regiment, so we started off. I noticed that almost all of our escort wore at least one brilliantly colored medal on their greenish tunics.

We were introduced to the commander, a quiet, stocky man with jet black hair. We gave the Russians our autographs. They gave us theirs. The commander invited us to lunch.

Honor Guest

He said I was the first American woman he and his troops had ever seen, and he seated me in the place of honor on his right at the luncheon.

Then the toasting began!

When the Russians start toasting, it is serious business. We drank toasts in cognac. Then toasts in wine. Then toasts in vodka. There was one other liquor which I could not identify but which tasted very much like straight grain alcohol.

I am afraid this historic meeting would have ended in blackout for everybody, but luncheon was served just in time. It started with creamed sardines and then highly seasoned meat patties. Many plates of hard-boiled eggs were passed and also plates of raw eggs. The Russians would break one end of the shell of the raw eggs and then suck the yolk and white out.

After luncheon we talked with the Russians for about an hour and then decided to cross the river to our lines again. Our trip back was made in what apparently had once been a racing shell used by some German sportsman. We pulled the shell up the river quite a distance because we did not want the current to sweep us down against a wrecked bridge. There were supposed to be two unexploded mines there.

The Russians ran to help us. They picked me up, put me in the shell and gave it a push. It was too hard a push and the shell half overturned, pitching me into the Elbe. When I climbed back in the shell I saw that some of my notes, which I had carefully taken in ink, were blurred.

When we got back to the American lines we heard a strange story that the man who actually captured Torgau was not an American or Russian soldier, but an Irish sergeant of the British Army. It seems he had been a prisoner of the Germans, had escaped and had taken possession of a bottle. After doing justice to the bottle he decided to walk into Torgau and buy a gift for his wife whom he had not seen for a long time.

Sgt. David T. Colin of St. Louis, another prisoner of war, told the story.

"We prisoners had taken over control of Fort Zinna, which was Germany's largest military prison. All the German guards except one left town on Monday, and he turned the administration over to us."

Uniform Is Enough

"This Irishman got hold of some cognac somewhere and decided to go into town and buy his wife a present. He was weaving and marching down the street and when the German civilians saw his British uniform they figured the Allies had arrived and began putting out white flags. About that time we saw the first American jeep roll into town. It turned out to be the lead jeep of the 69th Division's patrol."

At that time the Russians were still on the eastern bank and the Americans decided to try to signal to them.

"They got a sheet from one of our prison beds," Colin said, and painted a crude American flag on it. The Russians across the river saw it and fired colored flares. We had no flares to fire back, so the Russians opened up in our direction with artillery. For a few minutes it was a pretty shaky time, but I guess the Russians saw the jeeps coming into town about that time because they soon stopped the firing."

Colin said 76 German officers, including five generals, had been held in the Fort Zinna prison, most of them because they were suspected of having been involved in the attempt on Adolf Hitler's life.

"They had been executing them at the rate of five and six daily," Colin said. "The last one executed was a Gen. Von Davis who was charged with deserting to the Serbian partisans.

"Six of the Americans in the prison were under sentence of death and five others were on trial for planning treason against the Reich."

FRAU HIMMLER MAINTAINS SHE IS STILL PROUD OF HER HUSBAND

by Ann Stringer, United Press Staff Correspondent.

Internment Camp on Rome's Outskirts, July 13. (UP)—Frau Margarete Himmler maintained today that she was still proud of her infamous husband and shrugged away the world's hatred of the dead Gestapo chief with the calm observation that no one loves a policeman.

When I told her that husband Heinrich had been captured and had died from his own dose of poison, Frau Himmler showed absolutely no emotion. She sat, hands folded in her lap, and merely shrugged her shoulders.

Until then she had not known what had happened to Himmler since he last telephoned her from Berlin around Easter while she was at their home near Munich.

When first captured by the Fifth Army she had claimed a weak heart and internment camp officials, fearful of a heart attack, never told her of her husband's death.

But even when I told her that Himmler was buried in an unmarked grave Frau Himmler showed no surprise, no interest. It was the coldest exhibition of complete control of human feeling that I have ever witnessed.

I talked to Frau Himmler in a luxurious villa home owned by a former movie magnate where she and her 15-year-old daughter, Gudrun, are being held with one other female internee.

I asked her if she was aware of her husband's activities as Gestapo chief and she replied, "Of course."

Then I asked her if she knew what the world had thought of him and she replied, "I know that before the war many people thought highly of him."

Asked if she realized that Himmler was probably the most despised and hated man in the world after the European war got well under way, Frau Margarete shrugged and said, "Maybe so. He was a policeman and policemen are not liked by anyone."

Frau Margarete denied the possibility that her dead husband might have been considered the No. 1 war criminal. She said, "My husband? How could he be when Hitler was fuerher?"

Asked if she was proud of her husband, Frau Margarete replied, "Of course, I was proud of him." Then she added, "In Germany wives would not even be asked such a question."

Then pressed as to whether or not she was still proud of Himmler when he had sentenced millions of innocent people to death by torture, gassing, or starvation, Frau Margarete answered non-committally, "Perhaps. Perhaps not. It all depends."

NOTES

1. Leonard Lyons, "Clips from Loose-Leaf Notebook," (newspaper article, but no other information available).

2. Art Chapman, "Defiant Reporter Got Story," *Fort Worth Star-Telegram*, 21 April 1985.

3. Barney Oldfield, *Never a Shot in Anger* (New York: Duell, Sloan and Pearce, 1956), 194.

4. Chapman, "Defiant Reporter."

5. Ann Stringer, "The Enemy Has Been Cut in Two: Texan Found Herself at the Front Lines of History," *Fort Worth Star-Telegram*, 21 April 1985.

2

Iris Carpenter

The letter to the editor said, "Tell that party who wears pants and signed himself 'R'—the one who criticized Iris Carpenter—to go lie dead somewhere. No one will miss him. I think Iris Carpenter ranks with Ernie Pyle and we readers of the [Boston] *Globe* would miss her the way we did Ernie."[1]

That wasn't the only letter the *Boston Globe* received in March of 1945 about Iris Carpenter, the reporter. One reader wrote, "She has excellent powers of observation and gives a clear report of what she sees."[2] Another reader had equally strong sentiments in response to statements that Iris had no business reporting earthshaking events. "That is certainly a very cool assumption on the part of a person who seems to be much prejudiced in favor of men. For this person who honors men when they take their lives in their hands at the front, evidently does not honor a woman who does the same thing."[3] That reader went on to say that the soldiers aren't complaining, nor are they usually nauseated by the sight of a beautiful girl, "even if she is also brave and clever." The letter also stated that since Ernie Pyle left the western front no one else but Iris Carpenter has made the stories live in such a heartfelt way.

Another letter to the editor concluded with, "My advice to 'R' is to pipe down." According to this reader of the *Boston Globe*, Iris Carpenter was second to none in reporting the war, and again compared her to Ernie Pyle: "She has made several scoops of real news that men missed, because of her daring, enthusiasm, originality and scorn of personal comfort," the letter said.[4]

These weren't the only letters responding to the anonymous "R." Some conjectured "R" was a jealous female, others thought "R" had to be a woman-hater. Letters came from both men and women readers

Iris Carpenter. Photo courtesy of Iris Carpenter.

of the *Boston Globe* and included statements such as "No writer . . . holds a candle to Miss Carpenter for giving us a stark and really inspiring picture of what our boys are going through right up at the front,"5 and "Wish we had more like her."6

Iris Carpenter was born in England. Her interest in newswriting began early, as a film critic for the London *Daily Express*. She served under Arthur Christianson with this newspaper until she married Charles Scruby. Then she stayed at home to raise a family—until war hit England and five German planes were shot down in the woods behind her home. She returned to work as a reporter for the *Daily Express*, and the London *Daily Herald* subsequently borrowed her. She experienced the phony war in London (1940), drove an ambulance through London blitzes and fires, and covered bombings in dozens of places, including Portsmouth and Southampton.

Then in 1942 it became apparent that the Allied armies would carry out a major invasion. Iris applied for accreditation with the British Expeditionary Force, but met with the attitude that women could stay home and cover the blitz but could not move with the armies to France. Determined to bypass that decree, Iris got the idea of becoming an American newspaperwoman and accompanying the American armies in the invasion. She met with Carlyle Holt of the *Boston Globe* and overnight was accredited to the First Army.

In her book relating experiences as a war correspondent, Iris wrote, "The only chance a newspaper girl had of talking to troops was by touring camps with the Red Cross doughnut girls."7 She described the preinvasion scene vividly—hedges snowed with May blossoms camouflaged stacks of ammunition, bluebells in the woods contrasted with the Red Crosses on tents and ambulances waiting for the wounded of the invasion. "Every tree and hedge played its part in the great camouflage. Woods and hedgerows were spiky with guns and jammed tight with vehicles. Towns and villages bristled with men and armor and equipment. Yet from the air southeast England looked as unmenacing as Maytime."8

On D-Day plus four she became one of the first women to land on the airstrip—just a slice of sand—in France. For a time the Savoy in London became press headquarters for reporters who commuted back and forth from Normandy. Transmission of stories in France was available only to correspondents who had accompanied the invasion troops. Others had to go back to London and fight to get their copy through. Iris called this "combat," which included getting through skirmishes in which no holds or tactics were barred. She wrote, "British and American War Departments differed officially in their attitude toward the most horrific of all the horrific developments of modern war—the woman war correspondent. The British War Office, voicing the dictates of Monty, who regarded women in the field as bad luck, bad business, and something to be scotched vigorously as an enemy advance, said flatly, 'We will not tolerate them.' "9 Americans, Iris discovered, were usually willing to allow women to report the war, and felt certain phases of the war were better covered by women. They issued uniforms, inoculations, the simulated rank of captain, and the status of war correspondent. There were generals like Patton who were determined to make gender an issue in war reporting, but Iris usually found Americans much more tolerant than the British War Office.

For a while life was a fantastic hodge-podge, Iris said, between rocket-bombed London and shell-rocked Normandy. When she did not return to London at night, she usually stayed on the Liberty ships, but even there it was hard to sleep because of the German air raids.

Back in London for story filing, soon after her first foray into Normandy and the surrounding area, Iris received a summons for court-martial. There had been a violation of order, SHAEF (Supreme Headquarters Allied European Forces) said. Apparently orders were issued for the beachhead and Iris was not to leave that area. She, however, went to Cherbourg, without proper military escort and without reporting to the port commander. She was threatened with disaccreditation. Iris gave her accusers her orders—typed in triplicate as always, something she didn't understand since she never needed to part with any sets. Discussion on what actually was the beachhead took place, and finally a definition came up—four miles inland from Omaha to Cherbourg. A relieved Iris left the London Ministry of Information, and the next day SHAEF changed their policy regarding beachhead visits for women, since they feared the entire western front would be overrun by females with typewriters.

Soon after Iris's encounter with SHAEF, women correspondents were placed under the authority of the Public Relations Division. They had permanent orders for a month, and could write about WACs, hospitals, and subjects the PR division said were desirable. They were not to go any farther than nurses or Red Cross girls.

Further difficulties plagued women war correspondents. The average correspondent usually stayed with camps that had jeeps, drivers, teletype and radio transmission, and censors in residence. Briefings were held twice a day. Women, however, were assigned to hospitals, which ironically were often nearer the enemy lines than the press camps. Women weren't supposed to leave these hospital areas, so they had little if any access to the press camp, no driver (they had to beg and cajole for jeep, driver and/or escort), and their copy didn't receive the attention that copy from a press camp did. In short, women correspondents, as a nuisance, would soon be a dying breed—or so thought SHAEF.

This did not deter Iris. She did report on the hospitals and sent her newspapers some excellent accounts about the wounded and the nurses, as well as her impressions of French and American hatred for the Germans. However, she didn't give up fighting for her stories wherever she saw them. As a *Boston Globe* story put it in 1945, after the war, "For months she was one of a small group of women correspondents who fought for their right to use the press camps on the same basis as the male correspondents and she finally shared in the victory for feminine rights. Since that victory she has stayed regularly with 1st Army."[10]

Iris could report the war as astutely as any of her peers, male or female. She also had an extra touch; she saw the unusual and reported it in sensitive writing that could stir the most hardened. As she was driving from Pont Hebert into St. Lô, she came across a dead American soldier lying under a fuchsia bush in full bloom. She wrote:

> He was lying on his face in a gateway with his legs tucked into his muddy combat boots that had scuffed the sand a bit before they stayed still. A coat over the top of him had sagged into the contourless, sun-dried mush. Hopping around him was a large, tame, white rabbit that had somehow escaped from the general holocaust. Browsing beside them was a donkey. Had it been his own home, the futility of it might have seemed less pitiably futile. But the few yards of gateway this man had fought and died so untidily meant nothing to him.... And for those few yards that could never benefit or matter much to his own country, or to those dear to him and to whom he was dear, he had to die.[11]

Iris followed the army through Caen, across the River Orne, and around Falaise. By the end of July the Americans knew the beginning of the end had come in the overall battle for France. Iris wrote from Vannes about French heroism and patriotism that she observed midst all the chaos. Most impressive were her accounts of local Frenchmen fighting against the Germans, thereby venting their fury at those years of mistreatment and subjugation, and worse. She called it "diabolical treatment," and "perverse deviltry of which Germans are capable before the benediction of death ended their sufferings."[12]

"Reporting such fighting was crazy, mad, and exciting, and quite dangerous. . . . One came on war any time any place, and the best one could hope for was luck enough to either by pass it or receive timely notice from the combatants."13 In these chaotic conditions Iris saw much to write about. She watched as in towns civil war broke out, and wrote about what the occupation really had done to the soul of Europe. It had made heroes and cowards, and created story-book characters out of people. It had bred hooliganism as well as heroism. They were ultra-everything, she reported—ultra-patriotic, ultra-fearful, ultra-excitable, ultra-suspicious. At one point she wrote, after being caught in a night of local combat, "No combat soldier, however experienced or well trained, did a better job of inching out in retreat with the fanny well down than this correspondent."14

Unexpected problems sometimes plagued her reporting. As the U.S. First Army moved toward the Seine, they were along the British army boundary, and sometimes wrong divisions got the credit for who did what along this march. She commented that one of her own BBC weekly broadcasts to America got a barrage of taunts from some G.I.s who came across her lying on her stomach under some apple trees, trying to make sense out of the fluctuating situation. She felt it was one of war's miracles that the Allies got to the Seine without fighting between the "Tommies and Joes!"

Then came the liberation of Paris, with all its exhilarating drama— and women correspondents, thanks to SHAEF, were denied this experience. They were rounded up and kept in the custody of a PR officer. Finally she got to Paris, and spent some time "hun-hunting" with the French liberation troops (Germans who hadn't left Paris were still embroiled in combat). She called this adventure "head-spinning," "a wild car ride and a fantastic half-hour of creeping into houses, up precipitous staircases, and in and out of attics, onto and across roofs, each of which seemed more terrifyingly dizzy-making than the last."15 The adventure included the muffled outburst of a Frenchman into whose bedroom she and her French escorts crept—"Is there no sanctuary," accompanied by an epithet. In the end, she couldn't even file the story like it was but had to settle for an innocuous dispatch.

From Paris Iris went toward Brussels, but soon had to return to Paris because an eardrum was shattered at the bombing of St. Lô. The eardrum became infected and she came close to a case of mastoiditis. There she had two worries—that an operation for mastoid might be necessary, and that the war would be over before she could catch up with it again. So when her hospital was to move into Holland with the Ninth Army, other patients were left behind but not Iris. As a *Globe* article, written about her when she arrived in the United States in 1945, said, "She figured that she could stay with the hospital and thereby continue medical treatment for her bum ear and at the same time be close enough to the war to cover it without too much trouble."[16] Her description of moving with a hospital resulted in much picturesque reporting, including features on nurses. She wrote about how Americans coped with their wounded, and how the wounded themselves behaved, and described incidents that showed Americans had a sensitivity toward people, especially the suffering.

Iris covered the battle of Arnheim, a tragic loss that meant the war effort would continue through the winter and spring, with all its accompanying horror. The army, and Iris with it, went on to Antwerp and Aachen, and then General Bradley issued instructions that were to take Americans on to the Rhine. During this movement, she wrote from near Metz about the bleak area with more than usual ugly debris of war in evidence. Her sensitivity in writing was evident: "Time was taken out to bury the men, but carcasses of cattle were everywhere. I don't know why the sight of a flock of sheep bowled stiffly on their sides, or a cow with the soft, flabby folds of her neck stretched taut to the sky, or a horse with his four legs jutting from a bloated belly, should seem more sadly to highlight the horridness of war than anything it does to men. I know only that it did. Maybe it's because animals are so unresponsible for it all."[17]

As the Germans retreated ahead of the Allied armies, they frequently left snipers and spies. Often the command, "Keep your head down," would be heard as Iris moved with her party. After one strafing by snipers near Metz, her driver was shot in the hand. As they cared for the wound, one thing distressed him more than his injury. "If SHAEF hears about Carpenter being in this show, they'll discredit her so fast it'll make her head swim," he said.[18] Her colleagues advised her to write the day's story without references to the violence they had encountered.

Then came the battle of Hurtgen Forest. By now Iris was accredited to the First Army. Few, she was to report, could have anticipated the enormous costs of this futile massacre. She wrote of the suffering of man and beast. At one point the wounded were herded into a barn, while the battle raged around the area. "Every time another crash shook the trembling structure, the surviving animals burrowed into the hay among the wounded, squealed and whinnied and bleated. A youngster with a dangling bloody mess of coat-sleeve where his left arm should have been had the other one firmly around a frightened pig. 'Silly, isn't it?' he cracked. 'Me, with pork my favorite meat!' "19 By now the American soldier, who had taken war in stride, felt real hatred for the enemy and the tone of the fighting changed.

It was during this time she met the man who would eventually become her husband. After a long, hard day, she pondered what sort of story she could write that wouldn't be blue-penciled by the censors until it wouldn't be worth anything, when someone asked, "What sort of a day have you had?" She gave him a rather ungracious reception— after all, she was hungry, had mud on her face, and hadn't had time to comb her hair. The man turned out to be the operations officer for the First Army.

The first phase of the Battle of Hurtgen Forest ended, and the Battle of the Bulge began. The official press camp was at Spa, at the Hotel Laaken. Some correspondents stayed at the Portugal. Then reports came that the Germans were fighting hard, and retreat might be necessary. Retreat they did, with the First Army headquarters, to Tongress. Iris had many close calls, and commented that it was tough for correspondents; but no matter how tough, nothing could adequately describe what the soldiers suffered. She described the suffering vividly, however, and commented, "For the first time the Yank soldier was not in the war to settle somebody else's grievance. He had one of his own, and he was mighty sore and plenty mad."20

Finally battle conditions became such that headquarters could return to Spa just a month after their undignified retreat. The press was briefed that the "bulge" would be bent into Germany, and the goal was Bonn. Iris went with the army's advance, of course, and wrote poignant accounts of the suffering of the soldiers as well as the people in the areas of conquest. She always mingled with the soldiers and knew what they felt. As she said, "There are times when the biggest story in the world dwarfs to insignificance against just one reaction of any ordinary person."21 The misery of cold, ice, snow, mud, lack of food, pain, frustration, and anger were vividly depicted as she wrote— as well as heroism, caring, and excitement.

On to Dueren and Cologne went the advance. The press camp stayed at Spa and the correspondents made the three-hour trek daily. Iris wrote about the smashed villages and the refugees. "They were Germans, but that made them no less pitiable; as, crying bitterly, pushing the sick and those too small to walk in perambulators and trucks, and dragging what few possessions they had managed to grab in the half-hour given them to leave home, they stumbled along to various collecting points."22 She told of a farmer, his wife and daughter, who looked at the scene and decided that the shame of Germany was too much to bear. She and her colleagues found the three dangling from ropes with chairs kicked out from under them; from a fourth rope hung their dog.

Cologne was taken, and then it was on to the Rhine and the bridge at Remagen. Here Iris would experience the first crossing with the Allied forces, and subsequently write about "her greatest thrill," as she put it. She and some colleagues were crossing the bridge to the eastern side of the Rhine, and about six times they had to jump out of the jeep. One shot shattered the windshield. She then realized that her jeep was the target of fire![23] Back at Spa, fifteen hours later, they filed their stories, only to have them pared down by the censors.

The press camp moved the next day. The greatest story of the war, the breakup of Nazi Germany, started to move so fast it was difficult to keep up with. She began covering the story by cub plane, when she could get one. During one flight, she spent three hours in a storm that buffeted them unmercifully, made two forced landings, got lost over German territory, and finally landed on the home strip with just enough gas left to fill a cigarette lighter. But that trip did give her a panoramic view of the war scene.

Telling the story of the war became as difficult as it had been during the Battle of the Bulge because the battle raced in all directions. She wrote movingly of seeing the people who were freed by the fall of Germany—the Poles, Czechs, Russians, French, Dutch, Belgians, Norwegians, and Danes. They needed everything from clothes to transportation, but they moved on, away from their imprisonment. She pondered about what war did to people and wrote, "The fact remains that war changes all it touches."[24]

Then came the most sobering part of the war, the overrunning of the concentration camps, first Nordhausen, then Buchenwald, and after that Dachau and the rest. She described the scenes of death and the horrors of the camps. She and two colleagues drove to a camp of hundreds of wooden huts which stood adjacent to a factory where warheads were assembled. She and the others entered a room where, in the final stages of starvation, lay forty people. She had to admit that the frightful conditions she had heard about were true.

Finally, the great merger of the Allied armies with the Russians was to take place. Iris was at Torgau, and took part in the impromptu celebration. After that first day, however, the press was barred, and the boundary crossed by invitation only. This, she said, was easily the worst experience of the war.

Then the war was over, on May 8. She sat at a press camp in a small hotel in Weimar and with her colleagues wrote the last dispatches.

Iris came to America on June 3, 1945. Her former boss, Carlyle Holt, had written an article about her, entitled "Even More Attractive than Photo, Says Holt." He described her as five feet six or seven, slender, blonde, blue eyes, with a mouth full of white teeth. He guessed she would weigh between 118 and 125. He commented on her neatness, whether in civilian clothes or in uniform. But then he went on to say, "I think she is made of whalebone and India rubber for endurance and a liberal dash of bulldog determination to get her where she wants to go, come what may."[25] Iris was already famous to the *Boston Globe* readers, and when she arrived she herself got excellent coverage. She said, commenting on seeing the famous New York skyline for the first time, "I was afraid that the sensation of combat would deprive me of the quality of being excited about anything else, . . . but I am excited."[26]

Iris married Col. Russell F. Akers, Jr., on January 20, 1946. After three years of separation, she had divorced her husband in England, a wealthy London real estate operator. Her son joined her, and her daughter stayed in school in England. "Red" Akers was with the War Department by then. Iris continued to write for some time, then worked for the Voice of America. She stayed with government work after that.

When she wrote her book, documenting her experiences as a war correspondent, she dedicated it to "First Army's Operations Officer 'Red' Akers (my husband), in acknowledgment and appreciation of all he has done to integrate 'No Woman's World' into the military background of war in Europe." Given Iris's own set of experiences, one might say she herself made it a world of woman's achievement rather than a "no woman's world."

SAMPLE OF WAR REPORTING BY IRIS CARPENTER

FIRST GIRL WAR CORRESPONDENT TO CROSS RHINE AT REMAGEN
GLOBE WRITER RECALLS "HER GREATEST THRILL"

Shell Smacks Iris Carpenter's Jeep Crossing River with 1st Army

By Iris Carpenter. (Globe Special War Correspondent) WITH AMERICAN 1st ARMY TROOPS ACROSS THE RHINE,

March 8—Read that wonderful dateline again, please—"with the American 1st Army Troops across the Rhine." We are over. And in strength. At long last that last great river we had to cross flows behind us! Our first troops were on the eastern Rhine bank at 3:50 yesterday afternoon. Ever since, strong forces of infantry have been surging over to establish a bridgehead which is extending every hour.

One of Greatest Stories of All Time

Once in every journalist's life there is a story that is such a thrill and privilege to tell that anything and everything the getting costs is more than worthwhile. Such a story is today's.

Though it meant getting up at 4 a.m. to jeep through driving rain and spewing mud for 13 hours, getting pinned down under .88 fire, having the wind screen of my jeep splintered by shellfire, getting sniped at, and finally, having crossed the Rhine I am unable to tell you anything but the barest bones of narrative until the security blackout is lifted somewhat.

I can only promise that when detail is possible, it will be one of the greatest stories of all time, not just of this war.

It began yesterday when, driving through toward the Rhine River south of Cologne, we reached the banks to find the situation was not as we had expected to find it.

Resistance was not the type we expected—it was such, in fact, that the troops called upon their commanding officer for a discussion. He heard what they had to tell him. He put his field telephone back in its leather case with a terse: "I'll be right down, boys."

The conference—in the street of as picturesque a Rhine village as ever decorated a wine label—lasted a matter of minutes. Then the first Allied soldiers to set foot on the far banks of the blue river, which is anything but blue in March, whatever it may be at other times of the year, were on their way to take the first German village on the eastern shore.

Infantry First Over

The first men over were the infantry with a few engineers. They were led by 1st Lt. Carl Timmeran, of Nebraska, and they met comparatively little resistance in the first phase of the operation.

There were small-arms fire, but such enemy as we were mainly concerned about were themselves too busy getting across the river to do anything else. They were all Nazis trying to make their way out across the Rhine from Schnee Eifel, where our converging 1st and 3d armies have them practically surrounded.

In fact, the prisoners we took this afternoon on our side of the river were just being waved on by Doughboys to wander alone into their cages, past the tide of Allied vehicles that flowed along the last roads in Europe over which the enemy expected them to come. They were roads much too narrow, seemingly, much too shelled, much too bad for the weight, the power and material needed for such an attack as ours.

Fast bulldozers, cranes and engineering equipment, with various other vehicles looking like lumbering prehistoric monsters rather than a supply train of modern war, were weaving their way today through road blocks, burned out tanks and trucks, over shell craters and towns so recently taken that we had not yet had time to pick up our dead or bulldoze more than mud tracks through the rubble.

We got jammed. We got ditched. Yet somehow or other our material got through to the other side.

NOTES

1. Fanny B. Oakes, "Letters to the Editor," *Boston Globe*, 28 March 1945.

2. A.M. Haywood, "Letters to the Editor," *Boston Globe*, 20 March 1945.

3. Mrs. John M. Goodnow, "Letters to the Editor," *Boston Globe*, 20 March 1945.

4. Jack Hazard, "Letters to the Editor," *Boston Globe*, 20 March 1945.

5. Mrs. J.J.F. Webster, "Letters to the Editor," *Boston Globe* , 20 March 1945.

6. Mrs. Deborah D. Moulton, "Letters to the Editor," *Boston Globe*, 20 March 1945.

7. Iris Carpenter, *No Woman's World* (Boston: Houghton Mifflin, 1946), 15.

8. Ibid.

9. Ibid., 32–33.

10. Carlyle Holt, "Even More Attractive Than Photo, Says Holt," *Boston Globe*, 19 April 1945.

11. Carpenter, *No Woman's World*, 58–59.

12. Ibid., 89.

13. Ibid., 82.

14. Ibid., 93.

15. Ibid., 117

16. Holt, "Even More Attractive."

17. Carpenter, *No Woman's World*, 170.

18. Ibid., 173.

19. Ibid., 192.

20. Ibid., 229.

21. Ibid., 248.

22. Ibid., 260.

23. Iris Carpenter, "Globe Writer Recalls 'Her Greatest Thrill,' " *Boston Globe,* 9 December 1948.

24. Carpenter, *No Woman's World*, 290.

25. Holt, "Even More Attractive."

26. John Barry, "Iris Carpenter Gets First Glimpse of U.S.," *Boston Globe,* 4 June 1945.

3

Ruth Cowan

"We were unloading in Casablanca," Ruth Cowan recalled, "when the explosion with Wes Gallagher occurred. He didn't want any women on his staff. I heard him say, 'Put them on the boat and send them back.' It upset me very much." By the time Ruth reached Algiers, her first assignment as a war correspondent, she already was an experienced and respected reporter, with other types of battles behind her, so this welcome certainly was upsetting.

Ruth Baldwin Cowan was born in Salt Lake City, Utah, in 1902 and graduated from the University of Texas in Austin in 1923, having concentrated on studying English, philosophy, and psychology. She taught at the Main Avenue High School in San Antonio from 1924–1927, then became a reporter for the *San Antonio Evening News* in 1928, writing general articles and features. She joined United Press and worked as the head of the bureau in Austin under the name of R. Baldwin Cowan. All went well until a UP official called long distance and asked to speak to the bureau head. She replied, "Speaking," and he told her that UP didn't have any women. Baldwin was fired.

Ruth then wired the general manager of Associated Press and asked if she could have a job; she said she had just been fired because she was a female. The general manager wired back that she was to report to Chicago where they were looking for a woman. Because the wire came on April Fool's Day in 1929, she thought it was a joke and even went so far as to have the wire confirmed. Ruth stayed with them for many years, first working in Chicago, where she wanted to cover gangster stories—she accomplished this and eventually covered the trial of Al Capone. In 1940 she moved to Washington and was assigned to mainly do women's stories. This, however, wasn't a confining job for Ruth, because if she wanted to write political stories, she could get information from politicians whose wives she knew well. She wanted to cover the press conferences of President Roosevelt, but her efforts were strongly opposed. She appealed to Eleanor Roosevelt, who then decided to have her own press conferences and speak to women reporters only. This was effective, since Mrs. Roosevelt frequently made headlines.

Ruth often accompanied Mrs. Roosevelt on speaking trips, and she also wrote about the Department of War (now the Department of Defense). "There were so many people to write about that I just got interested about the war," she recalled. She requested AP to send her to Europe; her acquaintance with Mrs. Roosevelt helped, and she received an assignment to go to London in 1942.

Her ship left from New York, and she shared a room with five WACs. She was in WAC uniform because she thought they would be near enough to a staging area. Before the trip was over, however, she discovered London would not be her destination, in spite of the fact that she had been issued woolen underwear. Her ship unloaded at Casablanca in Morocco, and the eventual destination was Algiers. "Our welcome was that we were very unwelcome," she remembered. "I was badly hurt, as they say, and didn't know exactly what I was supposed to do. We were dumped in a warring country, yet our own people were against me. I didn't know where I would find my next meal, or where I would sleep. But I stuck it out."

Ruth was not deterred from carrying out her duties. By now she was an experienced reporter, so she wrote some stories that first night, wondering how she would file the material. The stories were about the WACs whom she had interviewed on the way over. Then she found something to eat and a place to sleep, and wondered what would happen. Someone said to her, "Don't worry, they will be glad to have you here," so she "settled down to take it." She began to write stories about the area, leaving the hard military news for her male colleagues so they couldn't claim she had ruined their military career. She did attend press conferences, and eventually wrote some material on military action. Later Ruth heard that someone had complained about the women reporters to General Eisenhower, who replied, "What's the matter? The women are doing a job; let them stay."

While in Algiers she met Inez Robb, although they did not work together. "She would go to one place and I would go to another. I would think of a good story and go get it. I did a great deal of my own assigning." One of these self-assignments was to get herself invited into a sheik's harem near Rabat, Morocco's capital. It was one coup men couldn't manage, because they were rebuffed when they made the same request.

One story Ruth told about herself involved her nervousness at wanting to remain a "natural blonde," largely because that's how her passport had her listed. An Algiers hairdresser worked on her hair, and it changed into a vivid purple. Only a large dose of sweetened lemon juice managed to undo the damage, but her major problems weren't over the rinse. Bees were attracted to the sugar in her hair.

After three or four months in Algiers, Ruth was sent to London and she stayed there until the invasion of Europe. "The reception I got in London was very, very different from what I got in North Africa, I can assure you." She was sent around the countryside, particularly to cover American installations. In England she had one of her strangest experiences when she was accused of being a spy and consequently was grilled by the military police. Her credentials were carefully scrutinized, while she begged, "Don't shoot me before you find out who I am." Apparently someone had been impersonating her.

Shortly after D-Day she was flown over to get a load of wounded. From that hospital plane returning from Normandy Ruth wrote about a twenty-one-year-old peacetime mechanic who said, "Hurry up and get me well again. . . . I wasn't in there long enough . . . I've got a score to settle."[1] She wrote about the other wounded who wanted to show her pictures of their families and tell her what was important about home. Her story centered around the persons involved with the evacuation of the wounded from Normandy and beyond. After this first trip she managed to be permanently assigned to follow the U.S. armies. "I've always been around the front wherever it was happening," she remembered. "Sometimes it was scary. You never knew where you would be or sleep."

On July 13, 1944, she wrote, "On the Normandy Beachhead. Why anyone who is scared of the dark and scared of firearms ever got themselves into the mess I did, I'll never understand. But there I was at midnight trying to get a little shuteye in a tent in a field which I wouldn't dare walk across in daylight because of mines. I had said I wanted to go to war—and brother, I had it, as the British say. It started out very simply."[2]

Ruth had wanted to see the treatment of casualties firsthand, so she went over to Normandy on a Liberty ship. No woman, she thought, had done that, so she welcomed the chance. She and another woman reporter went ashore in the morning, climbing down a rope ladder over the side of the ship. It was to be a short stay, but then she discovered that if she wanted a story she would have to stay overnight, as no wounded were evacuated that day. Sleeping in a foxhole didn't appeal to her. "I don't like spiders and bugs that consider the earth theirs. For this softie they put up a cot in a spare hospital tent."3 Then she heard planes. It occurred to her that they weren't far from the front lines. The ground reverberated with the shock of bombs, so Ruth climbed out of her cot and under it, then put her helmet over her face. Finally, the noise subsided and she went to sleep.

At one point near Pont Hebert and St. Lô, she and Iris Carpenter were scouting around the battle zones for stories, then tried to get an ambulance lift back to the hospital they were traveling with. While they waited for transportation at the crossroads of St. Lô, an order to "hit it" came before the ride. They scrambled into a hole, then realized that Germans were bombing the crossroads because they were the main supply routes.

Ruth was perturbed because the shell hollow, as she called it, was overhung by a prison wall under which lay bodies of approximately fifty French political prisoners whom the Germans had abandoned to the bombings. She insisted there had to be a better hole, Iris remembered, while the military police who had ordered them to "hit it" kept insisting that undoubtedly there *was* a better hole, but now was not the time to find it. The wall didn't collapse and after the bombing Ruth and Iris again tried to thumb a ride with an ambulance. A command car of officers drove up; at first the officers were suspicious, then indignant. " 'You mean you two out here at this time of night are having to thumb your way back to your hospital!' they demanded. 'War correspondents don't have to do that sort of thing. They have their own jeeps and drivers.' 'Check!' Ruth answered. 'But we happen to be WOMEN correspondents.' "4

It wasn't easy for Ruth to carry out her duties as a war correspondent. Sarah McClendon wrote, "Ruth Cowan was one of a number of women war correspondents in World War II who had a rough time even staying in Europe. Ruth always was on the verge of being sent home when officials found her interviewing the top generals, Bradley included."5 When commenting on the material she sent to AP, Ruth said, "I wasn't out to defy orders, or find material that would be censored. I wrote what I felt should be written."

One of Ruth's dispatches to AP was from the U.S. Army medical station at the Fifth Army front lines. She wrote about two dentists who had rigged up "an efficient if novel dental office from a captured German official's horsedrawn trailer."6 The dentists had painted it white, and had a generator for light. Ruth concluded her report with, "They had a small desk in one corner where records are kept—but they don't send out bills."7

Ruth got to Paris and stayed at the press headquarters for several months while she did stories from all around France. She was also sent to Rome to join the House of Representatives Armed Services Committee traveling around Europe, taking a look at what was happening. She had covered Congress frequently, so AP thought she would handle this assignment well. The group was received by the Pope; during the audience Ruth took out a pencil and wrote down a few things, when she noticed the Pope was looking at her. She figured it must be against the rules, so she put her pencil away, and was rewarded by a most charming smile. "I've never seen anybody grin so widely as he did," she remembered.

Barney Oldfield recalls one of the strangest of wartime press conferences at which Ruth was present. The case involved "an American sergeant who had leaned too hard into his goodnight kisses when courting a British girl in the midlands. She gave birth to quadruplets."8 Since the sergeant was married, the press asked him what he thought his wife would do. "He intrigued them considerably by saying that he had written a letter of explanation, and that he was certain 'she will understand.' Such assuredness of wifely devotion under what seemed to be great duress made the sergeant extremely interesting to the London-based correspondents."9 Ruth paced the floor outside of the room where the press meeting was held, trying her best to hear. " 'Why don't you go in and take a seat?' I [Oldfield] asked her. 'No, thank you!' she said, shying away. 'I wouldn't risk breathing the same air with him.' "10

During Ruth's two and a half years as a war correspondent, she met with some of the major figures of that time, including Generals Dwight Eisenhower, Omar Bradley, and George Patton, and covered some of the major battles including the Battle of the Bulge.

Ruth returned to the United States a few days before V-E Day, and after some time off to rest, she joined the Washington bureau of AP. She covered the House Armed Services Committee as well as the White House and the Capitol. When she married Bradley D. Nash, at that time undersecretary of commerce, in 1956 she retired from AP. Bradley Nash was in public service for many years and is presently mayor of Harpers Ferry, West Virginia, where the Nashes live. He is also the author of several books, including *Staffing the President*.

Ruth Cowan was one of those women war correspondents who had a credible career both before and after the war, with war reporting being just one in a series of major accomplishments in journalism. When Helen Thomas, White House bureau chief for UPI, spoke to an audience at Shepherd College early in 1987 she spoke of Ruth Cowan, saying, "She's ten thousand times better than I am." She wrote to Ruth, "I think we have a special bond fighting the good fight for women in journalism. . . . You were always a star to look up to . . . I still think that newswomen of that (our) era were outstanding, unique and strong. We had to be."11

SAMPLE OF WAR REPORTING BY RUTH COWAN

By Ruth Cowan. (Advance) . . . An American beachhead in Normandy, June 23–(AP)–Men newspaper correspondents have described its terror and tragedy and its human comedy, and strategists in and out of uniform have talked about tactics and their significance.

They know about such things. I don't.

But I do know how what this hard-won beachhead looks like to a woman.

As one of seven women war correspondents—the first in France—I tried to see what would mean the most to the women back home—to all the folks back home.

Primarily there is the American medical care of the wounded. That is why I went—to get the story firsthand—and it is a story to make all Americans proud.

We were flown by the Ninth Airforce Service Command's Transport Group, commanded by Col. Carl R. Feldman, Sabethan, Kans. These C-47's carried as much as 100,000 pounds of freight daily to France and brought out as many as 700 wounded in one day. They have gotten men back to hospitals in Britain 3 1/2 to five hours after they were wounded.

Pilot Lt. Art Stinnett, Sacramento, Calif., who taught shorthand in Phoenix, Ariz., to get money for flying lessons, invited me to ride in the co-pilot's seat. Engineer Sgt. Albert Yarbrough, El Paso, Tex., clamped phones over my ears. I heard the control order, "Take off southwest." At another field we transferred to a different plane bound for France.

The planes carry an army flying nurse and a medical technician. On ours were Sgt. Kenneth Warden, Stevens Point, Wis., making his fifth trip with Lt. Edith Brown, Port Huron, Mich., on her fourth.

With us also was Major William Jordan, squadron surgeon and a graduate of Emory University who practiced a number of years at Milledgeville, Ga. Capt. William A. Savin of Philadelphia, Pa., was our conducting officer. Lt. Lester Dale Skeets, Lansing, Mich., took the second plane off, with Lt. Edwin A. Erwin, Hattiesburg, Miss., as co-pilot. There was no riding in the co-pilot's seat for me now. We were to go close enough to see battle haze over the Cherbourg area.

Radio operator PFC Earl R. Palmatier, Amsterdam, N.Y., was tense over his instruments. Engineer PFC Frederic Hoaglum, Big Fork, Minn., watched for hostile aircraft. The unarmed C-47's sometimes have fighter cover; sometimes they don't.

Two fighters escorted us toward French fields neat and green, and we landed sharply on a strip laid down by detachments of this same transport group.

We were approached at once by soldiers curious about the new arrivals. They were tired and grim, saying little at first, yet wanting to talk. Their field uniforms were dusty, but they had found time to shave.

They watched and listened as you wrote one man's name and experiences in a notebook.

"Will the story be in my hometown paper?" was the closest any of them came to asking anything outright. They asked that because it is a way of letting the homefolk know they are safe.

It was the same with both men and officers. Among them were seaman second class John Dolan, West Orange, N.J.; Capt. Robert Mulligan, Capron, Ill.; and Warrant Officer Curtin Ferrell, Pontotoc, Miss.

Home things come first in their conversations with a woman correspondent, but they also are eager to know all about the flying bombs the Germans have been firing into southern England. Trucks come for the planes' loads and hurry off. Ambulances rumble up. Patients are quickly transferred to the planes—usually about 24 litters to each one—and the planes take off. It is not safe to linger.

Well-camouflaged is the tent of Major Milton Evans, Gulfport, Miss., Commander of Advance Headquarters, reached by crossing a clover field.

You stay in the path resisting the temptation to pick beautiful red poppies. There is a dull boom—and dust thrown high on the beach shows why. Mines are still being found.

Enroute to the holding station our ambulance driver, Private Albert L. McNally, Vine Grove, Ky., pointed to a clump of trees. He said, "A sniper hid there. It was days before we could get him out."

McNally came in on "D-plus-one." The first three days ashore he got no rest. "Couldn't take the time," he said.

A grand job is being done by all the litter bearers and ambulance drivers. A wounded soldier said to me, "Those medics"—first aid men and litter bearers who go into the front lines unarmed—"are grand guys."

"Over and over I've heard that 'every litter bearer should receive a citation,' " said Capt. Arthur Kleinman of Buffalo, N.Y., a dentist on duty as admissions officer at a holding station.

Capt. Walter Shepherd of Ososso, Mich., a surgeon, and Lt. Jack H. Mericle of Lima, Ohio, agreed.

"Many didn't sleep for 48 hours," Mericle said.

He didn't himself.

This holding station has really seen action. It came as three separate units D-Day afternoon. It is now consolidated under Lt. Col. George McShatko of Portland, Ore.

"Wounds were very bad the first days," Kleinman said, "as they were multiple. They are now less severe and there are more single wounds. We're beginning to get combat exhaustion cases, but not so many as expected."

Mericle said "Medical supplies have been wonderful. They didn't let us down."

The last planes were loading now and the time was short but I noted pup tents and slit trenches lately occupied by the Germans and the roofing on the adjoining Nazi dugout, where Kleinman and Capt. Walter Sielski of Buffalo, N.Y., live.

I said goodbye to Capt. J.W. Pace of Salt Lake City, Utah, in charge of all evacuations from France, and his associate, Capt. W.B. Oliver of Belvidere, Ill., who are aided by Capt. William C. Phillips of Richland, Ga.

Aboard the plane, Lt. Gertrude M. Berlings of Shelton, Conn., and Washington, D.C., and Sgt. Lora Pearman of Newport, Ind., medical technician, attended the patients.

Lt. Norman Corman of Woodstock, Va., was pilot and flight officer Leonard Ketner of Reading, Pa., was co-pilot on the return trip.

When they set the plane down in Britain patients not requiring immediate treatment were taken to a "transit" hospital. Patients needing further care are sent after a few days to general hospitals.

NOTES

1. Ruth Cowan, Associated Press dispatch, 23 June 1944.
2. Ruth Cowan, Associated Press dispatch, 13 July 1944.

3. Ibid.

4. Iris Carpenter, *No Woman's World* (Boston: Houghton Mifflin, 1946), 65.

5. Sarah McClendon, "The Stories of Women Journalists," *The Blade* (Toledo, Ohio), 17 November 1985.

6. Ruth Cowan, Associated Press dispatch, 1 January 1945.

7. Ibid.

8. Barney Oldfield, *Never a Shot in Anger* (New York: Duell, Sloan and Pearce, 1956), 38.

9. Ibid.

10. Ibid.

11. Helen Thomas, letter to Ruth Cowan, 19 January 1987.

4

Tania Long Daniell

"It was an exhilarating experience—a dramatic one. That's where the big story was," Tania Long said when reflecting on her years as a war correspondent in Europe. "I know I keep repeating the word 'exhilarating,' but that's what it was." Tania (her full name was Tatiana) was born in Berlin, Germany, in 1913 to a Russian-born mother and British father. Her father was a journalist who had gone to Russia before the turn of the century and had fallen in love with both the country and a Russian girl. The couple had settled in Germany, but when Tania was only a year old the family had to leave because of World War I. They moved to Scandinavia and eventually to the United States. After the war ended, they returned to Berlin and Tania's father became known for his knowledge of German finance and economics.

Tania attended German schools and studied in Paris and England as well, specializing in history and economics. She met her first husband, an American, in France and they were married in 1932. They had one son.

When the couple separated in 1936, Tania looked for work. An acquaintance told her about an opening on the *Newark Ledger* (now the *Star-Ledger*). Tania applied and admitted, "I have no experience, but I'm interested." She explained that her father had been a newspaperman and she knew what it was all about. The paper hired her, saying they were looking for someone to break in. She began at a salary of $18 a week.

At first she did rewrites and mundane items, but gradually worked to covering everything from the Newark Airport to the police department. Because the airport was the largest near New York in those days, many personalities and celebrities traveled through there. She covered court trials, politics, fires—general assignments that were to

Tania Long Daniell. Photo courtesy of Tania Long Daniell.

lay the groundwork for her later success as a foreign correspondent because of the variety of stories.

In 1938 she became concerned about the European situation because her parents were still in Berlin. She took a leave of absence and boarded a ship. En route she received a cable from her father that said, "Leave the ship at South Hampton and go to London. I will meet you there. Mother is in Bruges, Belgium." It really looked like war, Tania recalled later. Then, however, British prime minister Neville Chamberlain returned from Munich and declared "peace in our time," so the family once again went to Berlin. Soon after, her father died. Because her mother couldn't take the family's money out of Germany, Tania couldn't afford to send her to the United States. She decided to try to get a job in Berlin. "Frankly, that interested me much more than going back to that little paper [the *Newark Ledger*]," she said. "And I was, again, in the right place at the right time. The *New York Herald Tribune* chief was looking for an assistant. His assistant, a young Jewish woman, was going back to New York because of the situation in Germany."

Tania got the job, and it meant being "chief cook and bottle washer—doing everything." She kept the accounts, translated articles for her boss, and finally began to do some writing.

Then it began to look like war again. Czechoslovakia had been overrun and Poland was being threatened. Tania feared that she would endanger her mother's and son's lives by staying in Germany, so she requested to be transferred. The *Herald Tribune* said, "Fine, as soon as you are replaced we have a job for you in Paris." The family's flight was chaotic, but finally they arrived in Paris. After she received her official papers and other items she was required to have (such as a gas mask), she was told she would be sent to London temporarily. The London office was short on personnel.

Tania's vivid descriptions of the aerial bombings of London made front-page news at home. In 1941 she won the Newspaper Women's Club award for her stories about the sinking of a British liner transporting refugee children, about London's poor population, and about the bombings, especially of the Savoy Hotel where she resided. She was honored at a reception in April of 1941, when she had briefly returned to New York.

Her article about the torpedoed refugee liner began:

In one of the most tragic sea disasters of the war, 293 persons, including eighty-three children evacuated from England to escape Nazi bombs, lost their lives when a liner bound for Canada was torpedoed by a German submarine last Tuesday night 600 miles at sea. . . . Only 113 persons out of a total complement of 406 aboard the vessel . . . were rescued by British warships and landed last Friday at a northern British port.[1]

She told how one of the children's escorts, a kindergarten teacher, managed to get her fifteen charges into a lifeboat, then had to watch while all but one died of exposure. She also related the story of the survivors through the eyes of Elizabeth Cummings, fourteen years old, who swam to a lifeboat and clung to it through the night.

During the heavy bombing of Coventry, Tania worked for thirty-six hours at one time. She had completed her work at the London office by 1:00 A.M. and went to Coventry. Since she could find neither a hotel room nor food, she kept on working. Then she proceeded to Birmingham, which was also being bombed. Except for minimal snacks, she was without food for two and a half days.

Tania's *Herald Tribune* articles were also printed in London newspapers. In September of 1940 the *News Chronicle* printed her article on the bombing of the Brittany coast. She had written, "For three and a half hours last night the Royal Air Force showered high explosive and incendiary bombs on the French naval base and shipbuilding harbor at Lorient, on the coast of Brittany, during one of the most furious offensives against Fuehrer Adolf Hitler's invasion bases."[2]

One of Tania's articles was about a French foreign diplomat's meeting with Hitler at the latter's "eagle's-nest retreat, high atop a Bavarian Alp."[3] Few Germans had been privileged to see this "fantastic pavilion where the Fuehrer, in solitary retirement, communes with his Teutonic gods," Tania wrote.[4] The diplomat found his experience so fantastic he wondered if he was dreaming—tunnels, heavy brass doors, massive construction, immense panorama of the mountains—and conjectured whether this immense hideaway was the product of a normal mind or of a man who was tormented by fears.

The *New York Times* correspondent in London at that time considered newspaper work a man's job, but later he wrote, "She provided us with as much competition as any man in London." As Stein wrote, "[Raymond] Daniell, of the *New York Times*, was bombed out of his home and office in London but often drove through the ruined streets to check damage from the raids. One of his rivals was winsome Tania Long, of the *Herald Tribune*. But love won over competition and they were married during the war."[5] Raymond Daniell was a friend of Tania's boss. She remembered, "We began to see each other and got along very well. We eventually fell in love and decided to get married."

In the spring of 1941 they flew to Lisbon—a dangerous flight in a blacked-out plane that flew down the coast of France—and then boarded an American ship. They were married in November of 1941. Tania was also reunited with her mother and son, who had been in Ireland while she reported from London, and then were taken to New York.

After the Daniells were married, they returned to London. Tania resigned her position because the *Times* and the *Herald Tribune* were competing newspapers. At first she did free-lance work for the *Times*, but soon was put on the staff. "They realized they were very short-handed," she said. "The war was developing in many directions." There were eleven exiled governments in London by then, so Tania found much to report on. The Daniells worked very late during the day because of the difference between London and New York time. "It was an interesting, crazy life," she recalled, "an upside-down life. We worked late, slept late, then worked late again. Raymond complained that he never saw daylight anymore." But, Tania commented, a person can adjust to anything, and they even "adjusted very nicely to the bombings." As she had said earlier, when still with the *Herald Tribune*, "When one hears bombs coming close there is no time to do anything. One hasn't time to be afraid, that comes later." It was like living in a tropical climate, she explained, when one could expect the rains to come at a certain time every afternoon. The bombings usually started at 8:00 P.M.

Tania reported on the people who were bombed out and found temporary shelter in the subways. These living quarters were eventually organized by the government, with bunks, toilet facilities, and canteens. She also wrote about the people living in caves in Kent. These had been used to grow mushrooms, but people fled to them for safety, and the government organized these accommodations as well.

When censorship restrictions on the bombardment of London were lifted, Tania wrote a lengthy letter to the Sunday editor of the *New York Times* about what it was like to live through the blitz that involved the V-1, a buzz bomb. These unmanned bombs, she explained, could do a great deal of damage but worse was the psychological effect—an "instinctive resentment against a 'thing' with no man in it to try to shoot at."[6] Tania found these bombings harder to get used to, and when the bombings came, she alternated between running to the hotel room window to look and burying her head under the pillow if one came too close. Finally, the Daniells began sleeping in the shelter. In the *Times* office, Tania was the official bomb-spotter because her office was located where she heard them before anyone else. She said in her letter, "Life does go on, now pretty much as usual. . . . I notice with myself and others that now that the newness has worn off, we have all become a bit more fatalistic and go around less tensely aware of possibilities."[7]

Two weeks after D-Day Tania managed to get to France. Unfortunately she encountered difficulties there.

> When Doris Fleeson, columnist for the *Daily News,* and I arrived in Normandy, the army would not put us up in the press camp, but put me and Doris into two different hospitals, with the nurses. The press camp was all male and there were no latrines for women! The result, of course, was that we had an awful time keeping up with the news. We did mostly features and had to scrounge transportation. But it was an exhilarating experience.[8]

Tania wrote a story about the operation of the field hospital. During this adventure she sometimes slept with her tin hat over her head because of the shrapnel rattling down through the apple trees.

Then Paris was liberated. Luckily the Daniells were in London when they heard the news and caught a ride to Cherbourg. Raymond wanted to open the Paris bureau of the *New York Times*. By now Tania was working for the Sunday department, which was a separate operation, and she was anxious to get stories about Paris. One of her reports summarized German records captured by the British during the invasion. These told of a methodical plan by Germany to maintain control of France, but "Nazi strategy collapsed."[9]

Another report described the mood of Paris after the liberation. "Parisians suffered a lot during the years of occupation, but they have a facility to bound back, and to see them today it is hard to believe that anything has happened. Now, days after the Allied entry, Parisians are still excited and emotional whenever they come in contact with American or British troops."[10] Tania recounted the problems Parisians and the French in general faced because of the rapidity of the liberation and their years of domination by Germany.

The war ended while the Daniells were in Paris. They were allowed into Berlin approximately a month later. The Daniells covered the Nuremberg trials and Tania wrote articles on postwar Germany. One of her stories was about the problems of reeducating the German population. The Nazis, Tania wrote, retained control in education as well as government, and America was referred to as the enemy.[11] In another dispatch to the *Times*, Tania described the plight of the refugees. The refugees were cold, underfed, and living in overcrowded camps. Conditions, Tania said, were appalling.[12]

The Daniells returned to London in 1946 and remained there until 1953; during those years they continued to report for the *New York Times*. They came back to the United States in 1953 but were transferred to Canada where they continued to report as a team. A feature on the Daniells stated that they covered the *Times'* largest beat, which ran from Newfoundland on the Atlantic to Queen Charlotte Islands on the Pacific. Sometimes they ventured into the far north and wrote about Eskimos in the Arctic and trappers in the cold Canadian regions.

In 1963 they joined the *Times* staff in New York and reported on the United Nations. Raymond retired in 1967 and died in 1969. The Daniells had returned to Canada after his retirement and Tania worked for the National Art Center as public relations director until she retired in 1979.

Tania earned the respect of her peers, who praised her as being a leading war correspondent and woman of ideas. In 1986 another woman who wrote for the *Times* in London, Virginia Lee Warren Bracker, said, "She was one of the best." Tania took her responsibility seriously; when the New York Newspaper Women's Club honored women journalists for 1942, Tania wired a message and said, "We are all proud to wear our country's uniform."[13]

A SAMPLE OF WAR REPORTING BY TANIA LONG

83 CHILDREN ARE AMONG 293 DEAD AS NAZIS TORPEDO REFUGEE LINER; CANADA-BOUND VESSEL IS SUNK 600 MILES AT SEA, STORM BALKS RESCUES

Victims Had Fled Nazis' London Raids

Some Were Survivors of Earlier Sinking; Seas Smash Boats and Rafts

By Tania Long. From the Herald Tribune Bureau. Copyright, 1940, New York Tribune Inc.

London, Sept. 22—In one of the most tragic sea disasters of the war, 293 persons, including eighty-three children evacuated from England to escape Nazi bombs, lost their lives when a liner bound for Canada was torpedoed by a German submarine last Tuesday night 600 miles at sea, it was officially announced tonight. Only 113 persons out of a total complement of 406 aboard the vessel—which sailed Friday, the 13th—were rescued by British warships and landed last Friday at a northern British port.

The torpedoing occurred last Tuesday at 10 P.M. during a heavy gale which cut to a minimum the chances of saving more than a small proportion of the ship's human cargo. Most of the lifeboats and rafts lowered in the dark were smashed or spilled over by the tempestuous sea. The ship sank in half an hour, carrying down with her a number of children trapped below or killed in the explosion.

Of the survivors, thirteen were children, six of whom were traveling privately and not regarded as evacuees. Only seven evacuee children were saved. The survivors included eighteen women and eighty-two men. Among the adults were forty-five male passengers and white members of the crew and thirty-six Lascars (East Indians). Not a few of the adults were aliens who had been interned in Great Britain and were being transported to Canada.

First Toll Among Children

This was the first loss of life among children evacuated to over-seas homes under the British government's scheme. Under the plan 3,000 children have been successfully transported to safety in the dominions and the United States. During August an evacuee ves-sel—rumored to have been the Volendam—was torpedoed but did not sink and all 320 of the children on board were brought back to England safely.

Most of the children lost last Tuesday were from London, Middlesex and Liverpool. They were escaping from the terrors of Nazi air raids to find safety in the dominion across the Atlantic when a Nazi torpedo struck their vessel and sent all but thirteen of them to death. They had said good by to their parents the previous Wednesday.

Two of the lost children were making their second attempt to reach Canada. They had been among the 320 survivors of the vessel tor-pedoed in August.

Five of those lost were brothers and sisters whose homes in south-west London had been bombed the day before they left to join the liner. They had escaped the bombing by taking refuge in the family's "Anderson shelter."

Their father, James Grimmond, said today: "This is not war; it's sheer, cold-blooded murder. I'm going to join up again, and all I ask for is a front-line job."

Captain Stays, Is Lost

The captain, who stayed on the bridge until the last few seconds, dived overboard and was lost. His last words were: "Get into the boats and look after yourselves." Then a series of explosions shook the ship and she sank. . . .

EX-LINER FIGHTS WARSHIP AND SAVES BRITISH CONVOY

The Jervis Bay Goes Down In Flames, Her Guns Barking to the Last; 29 of 38 Merchantmen Escape; Berlin Said Raider Sank Them All

By Tania Long. London, Nov. 12—Sinking and afire from stem to stern but with her guns blazing to the last, the 14,164-ton armed British merchant cruiser Jervis Bay fought a German warship—believed to have been one of the 10,000-ton "pocket battleships," the Admiral Scheer or the Luetzow—at dusk last Tuesday, 1,000 miles out the Atlantic from the American coast, and enabled a convoy of thirty-eight merchantmen, bringing vital supplies from the New World, to scatter.

Twenty-nine of the freighters escaped, and twenty-four of these reached a British port today. The fate of the nine other ships in the convoy is uncertain. All may have been sent to the bottom after the destruction of the Jervis Bay. Among the surviving vessels were the 16,698-ton motor liner Rangitiki and the 4,952-ton Cornish City, whose distress signals last week were the first indications that a raider was active in the shipping lanes of the North Atlantic.

The German high command said the entire convoy had been destroyed, but the Jervis Bay, fighting as gallantly as the armed merchant cruiser Rawalpindi had done against the Deutschland (later named the Luetzow) last winter, sacrificed herself to allow nearly three-fourths of the vessels to escape in the gathering gloom.

Details of the action were told by some of the men who, aboard the freighters in convoy, watched the Jervis Bay steaming out from the line to meet the powerful raider. In peace time the Jervis Bay was an Aberdeen and Commonwealth liner plying between England and Australia, carrying freight and the poorest classes of immigrants.

British and foreign vessels in the convoy, eyewitnesses recounted, followed one another across a calm sea. It had been a perfect day. Just as darkness was gathering the silence was shattered by a distant explosion. Then came the scream of a shell from below the horizon. It fell harmlessly a few yards from the ship.

The shell was followed by another. Soon the silhouette of a warship emerged, and the firing grew more intense. Immediately the order to scatter was given, and, as the ships obeyed, the raider began to concentrate on the Rangitiki, the largest vessel in the convoy.

The raider stood off about seven or eight miles as she poured shell after shell in the direction of the Rangitiki. Suddenly when it seemed that the merchantman could no longer escape the devastating fire, the Jervis Bay steamed straight out in front of her, turned slightly and raced toward the attacking warship.

The crew of the Jervis Bay must have known that she stood little chance against the raider's superior armament, but they manned their guns and blazed away furiously, drawing the fire from the Rangitiki.

As the convoy of ships disappeared one by one into the safety of the night, the Jervis Bay fought grimly on. The battle did not last long. The Jervis Bay, battered from stem to stern, began to burn. Soon she was blazing. Still her last remaining gun could be heard barking defiantly between the thunderous explosions of the raider's heavy guns.

Full details of what happened then are not available. The Admiralty said that nearly two hours after the beginning of the engagement an explosion was seen aboard the Jervis Bay. Sixty-five survivors, the Admiralty added, were known to have been aboard a merchant ship.

The Jervis Bay was manned by officers and men of the Royal Navy Reserve. She was commanded by Capt. H.S.F. Feegan.

A British captain of one of the convoy ships, interviewed on landing today, said he thought the raider was a pocket battleship and believed the shells were fired from eleven-inch guns.

NOTES

1. Tania Long, "83 Children Are Among 293 Dead as Nazis Torpedo Refugee Liner," *Herald Tribune,* 22 September 1940.

2. Tania Long, "R.A.F. Fires Visible for 70 Miles," *News Chronicle* (London), from the *Herald Tribune* bureau, 13 September 1940.

3. Tania Long, "Where Hitler Lives Like a God," *Herald Tribune,* 6 January (no year, but probably either 1940 or 1941).

4. Ibid.

5. M.L. Stein, *Under Fire: The Story of American War Correspondents* (New York: Julian Messner, 1968), 101.

6. Tania Long, letter to Lester Markel, 9 July 1944.

7. Ibid.

8. Tania Long, letter to author, 11 November 1986.

9. "Supermen in a Dither," *New York Times,* 19 October 1944.

10. "Rebirth of France," *New York Times,* 2 September 1944.

11. "U.S. Occupation Fails to Break Nazis' Grip," *New York Times,* 25 April 1946.

12. "Refugees," *New York Times,* 21 November 1945.

13. "Newspaper Club Cites Reporters," *New York Times,* 15 May 1943.

5

Kathleen McLaughlin

In reply to the rather standard question, "Why did you want to go and report the war?" Kathleen McLaughlin, now ninety years old, answered firmly, "Who wouldn't! For heaven's sakes!" The experiences of being a war correspondent during World War II remained in her memory, even in view of a respected and eventful career before and after that era.

Born in 1898 in Greenleaf, Kansas, she moved at a very early age to Atchison and considered that her hometown. "Ever since she was old enough to read a paper she had the idea that she wanted to be a reporter."[1] She attended high school but did not graduate. When the one man who was a reporter for the *Atchison Globe* left for another job, Kathleen asked for the position and got it. She worked there for a year and a half, writing stories, "like one would write in a small town," she explained. "About everything and everybody."

In the early twenties, while on a summer vacation in Chicago, she went to the *Chicago Tribune* and took some clippings with her. It was a gamble but also a strategic moment. "She had a capable manner, a persuasive tongue. The city editor studied her clippings and told her she could go to work in the morning."[2] Kathleen made an impression when she managed to get an interview with Olgivanna Milanoff, who had been arrested with Frank Lloyd Wright and their illegitimate daughter. Olgivanna talked to Kathleen freely, and because curiosity regarding the brilliant architect was high, the story was read with eagerness and great interest. After this Kathleen specialized in crime reporting.

Kathleen had managed to be the right woman for the right moment in the past, and this was another fortunate time for her because the 1920s were an era when "machine guns rattled through the streets of Chicago with astonishing frequency and the overlords ran the town."[3]

She became acquainted with the major figures of Chicago's crime world and wrote stories about them. Once she was the one who had to tell a woman that her famous gangland husband had been killed.

"Miss McLaughlin interviewed the crime czar [Al Capone], chased Prince Nicholas of Rumania through the streets of Chicago, found Lady Diana Manners modest and Peggy Hopkins Joyce high-hat. She met the celebrities, freaks and criminals of the period."[4] She reported on a myriad of topics, from the life of a maid (she herself worked as one briefly to find out what it was like) to good eating in Europe. As women's editor for eighteen months she instituted an annual conference on current problems.

Kathleen's tenure at the *Chicago Tribune* came to an end suddenly. A new Sunday editor had been selected. He was her immediate boss, and to her utter astonishment accused her of trying to get his job. "There aren't many things you can say to that kind of charge. I simply wrote my last column and wrote out a resignation and handed both in. There's no way to keep on working with a man of that stripe," Kathleen said.

She moved to New York, and again was at the right place at the right time. The *New York Times* was going to start a woman's club page, and she was hired to edit it. But Kathleen was not confined to women's news. "I wrote everything in the world," she remembered. As Ishbel Ross wrote in 1936, "She now edits this page, covers women's conventions and does general news assignments, for she is a versatile and experienced reporter. Her stories on the political conventions of 1936 made the front page day after day. She is accepted in the city room on exactly the same basis as the men."[5]

Then World War II came and she wanted to report on the big story, so she joined the *New York Times* bureau in London. She had difficulty convincing the *Times* to send her, a woman, and didn't manage that until early in 1944. "I suppose their views moderated over the years, and in wartime things are not quite as methodical and calm as normally, so they allowed me to go," she recalled.

Her reporting began from London and proceeded to other military headquarters. She wrote day-to-day reports and sent them back to the *Times*. Among her stories were accounts of hospitals and the treatment of the wounded, the evacuation of Holland by the Germans, and finally the de-Nazification trials. Commenting on her war experiences, she said, "It was an unusual experience and memorable to say the least. Anything but routine."

During the war, she traveled with a group of war correspondents, following the U.S. forces wherever they went. She wore the regulation uniforms ("I didn't like them particularly"), ate K-rations ("didn't really have a food shortage—it was OK"), and lived wherever she was told to ("a hotel, or tent, or a big house taken over as a press camp"). One of the funniest, yet most difficult things, Kathleen remembered was moving from place to place and sleeping in all kinds of accommodations. Once it was a hammock, another time a bed with a hump-shaped mattress which gave her a funny sensation.

Another humorous event Kathleen recalled was that Russian soldiers who took over German homes removed the bathroom and kitchen water fixtures, thinking that would allow them to have running water at home! They didn't realize plumbing had to be behind the fixtures before they would produce the miracle of water running from the wall.

The most memorable experiences came after the war ended, however. These were the Nuremberg trials, and they made the greatest impression on her. She recalled that the trials took place in an old German palace just outside of Nuremberg, and were handled by the judiciary branch of the U.S. Army. Quarters for the press had been arranged, and she associated with journalists of several nationalities.

Kathleen's memory was keen regarding details of the trials. The judges sat opposite the prisoners' boxes and there were two Russians, two Americans, two British, and two French judges. She marveled at the humble behavior of the German attorneys. Kathleen stated she felt an immense curiosity about these trials and what took place, and she stayed for the full ten months.

Kathleen also covered the Berlin blockade and the occupation of Germany and continued to report from that country until 1951. Then she received an assignment to the United Nations in New York. She came back to the *New York Times* city desk and "picked up where I left off years ago." Her fame as a journalist increased as she reported from the United Nations for the *New York Times*, a position she held until she retired in 1968. She now resides in a nursing home outside of Chicago.

Kathleen McLaughlin has an excellent reputation as a first-class journalist. Her accomplishments in the field have been such that many who know her have been unaware that she reported from the World War II scene as a war correspondent. For her, it was just one more exciting experience during an exceptional career.

NOTES

1. Ishbel Ross, *Ladies of the Press* (New York: Harper, 1936; reprint, 1974), 161.
2. Ibid.
3. Ibid.
4. Ibid, 163.
5. Ibid.

6

Bonnie Wiley

"Why did those [censored] editors send me a WOMAN correspondent! Make up your mind, young lady. You'll be treated just like a man and you'll report just like a man and you'll contribute to AP stories just like a man. And no prima donna. No special treatment!" fumed Murlin Spencer, head of AP war correspondents. The object of his tirade was Bonnie Wiley, and as she later said, his "bark was beautiful but his bite was toothless." She added that any success she may have had as a correspondent was due to this man and his well-planned assignments for her.[1]

Bonnie Wiley was born in Portland, Oregon, and raised in Yakima, Washington. She started on the *Yakima Daily Republic* at the age of seventeen, right out of high school. Subsequently, she worked as a reporter-photographer on the *Portland Oregonian* and as a feature writer on the *Seattle Times*. Then she became western feature editor for Associated Press in San Francisco.

Bonnie became a war correspondent in January of 1945. "There was a big story breaking," she explained, "I wanted to cover it." Accredited to the navy and therefore traveling under navy orders, she wore a WAC officer's uniform with the navy insignia, but when she worked she wore G.I. suntans or dark-greens. She commented, "They didn't fit very well"; she looked too much like Gravel Gertie. When she left San Francisco for Guam, she weighed 118 pounds. By the time she returned after the war was over, about a year later, she was down to 97 pounds.

As the only woman war correspondent the Associated Press had in the Pacific theater, Bonnie found that war in the Pacific "definitely was not run on a co-educational basis." In Guam she stayed in the sentried area of the island commander instead of being quartered with the men correspondents at CinCPac Hill, about three miles away and con-

Bonnie Wiley. Photo courtesy of Bonnie Wiley.

venient to the area where stories were breaking constantly. When she wanted to go to CinCPac Hill, a jeep would have to pick her up or she would hitchhike. This held dangers, because Japanese soldiers were hidden in the hills of the island. One morning at dawn she was hitchhiking when she heard men's voices in a jungle ravine close to her path. She listened. They spoke Japanese! She turned and ran. "Had they been awarding Olympic medals, I would have won a dozen," she later wrote.2 After that she always waited for a jeep.

There were difficulties being a lone woman in a war area—and lack of powder rooms was one of them. When there was a nurses' area, Bonnie usually used their facilities. When there was none, a male war correspondent or an officer stood guard while she grabbed a shower. As she puts it, "Fun!" When she and AP photographer, Max Desfor, were on the same assignments, he did his duty by guarding outside doors. She could hear his worried voice, "You can't go in there. There's a woman in there," and hear the purple language from the swearing G.I.s. But Max stood his guard.

Places to stay varied. Once she bunked with some USO girls; once she stayed in an abandoned schoolhouse. She ate in the mess halls. While covering stories in Japan after the war she had the luxury of a postwar hotel.

"I was guarded and treated like the crown jewels too much of the time. Men, bless them, went out of their way to help me," Bonnie stated.3 "Men of the armed forces and men correspondents were all a great help to me."4 Were there advantages to being a woman in this setting? "Everybody wanted to help and did. And yes, a woman does stand out and gets lots of help—and gets remembered."5

But being treated like the crown jewels did not prevent Bonnie from turning out some fine reporting. She wrote features and covered hard news. She wrote about the start of the battle of Iwo Jima and went out to relieve Al (Red Dog) Dopking who had covered the Okinawa invasion. She covered the mop-up of the battle for Okinawa. For a while she wrote the AP column, "Dateline Pacific." "I did more features, as I had been western editor for AP Feature Service in San Francisco and was very much attuned to features."6

One of her stories came from aboard a transport plane over Okinawa on June 18, 1945. She watched as the battle reached its final stages after weeks of fighting. She wrote in picturesque detail about the panoramic view she had of the battle. Because she was removed from the noise of battle, she felt as if she were seeing a silent newsreel. "Broken clouds, like marshmallows, hung over the battle. . . . Diving and flying through the clouds were American planes like tiny specks on a white tablecloth."[7] The ships looked more like toys on a painted ocean. But it was no toy battle, she wrote, because before this flight she had talked with doctors and the wounded waiting to be taken to Marianas base hospitals. It was a real war. With this article Bonnie displayed her ability to combine feature elements with news of the event itself.

Toward the end of the war, an air corps pilot asked if he could bring her something from Hawaii. She wanted some cold cream to help the leather-looking skin she had acquired in that climate. She got her cream and was smearing most of it on her face when she heard shouts, "The war's over! The war's over!" Hirohito had made his announcement. And there she was, with cold cream lathered all over her face!

Bonnie was sent to Japan after the war ended and her first assignment was the POW camps. "I got some hair-raising stories from the ex-POWs," she said.[8] She went on to Manila to cover the arraignment of General Yamashita when the first war crimes trials started.

She returned to the *Portland Oregonian*, but after six months decided she had done everything once or twice before, so she went to college. She received her B.A. from the University of Washington and returned to newspaper work for five years as managing editor of the Yakima, Washington *Morning Herald*. Then she decided to enter teaching. She received her master's degree from the Columbia University Graduate School of Journalism, and her Ph.D. from Southern Illinois University. For ten years she taught at Center Washington University in Ellensburg, and for another ten years at the University of Hawaii. Bonnie then traveled to American Samoa and spent three years helping develop the college there, the American Samoa Community College. She returned to teaching part time at the University of Hawaii, where a special journalism program includes journalists from the People's Republic of China—twelve journalists at a time.

When the Korean War came along, Bonnie said, "No way; one war to cover in a lifetime is enough—maybe too much."

A SAMPLE OF WAR REPORTING BY BONNIE WILEY

JAPS CAN'T BEAT GOIN' JESSIE, JOHN D., CURLY

TINIAN.—(AP)—Of the many tough fighting teams in the B-29 league, there's one out here in the 313th Bombardment Wing that hasn't been beaten yet. It consists of John D., Curly, and Goin' Jessie. John D. is a pilot, Curly is his ground crew chief, and Goin' Jessie is their Superfortress.

Lt. John D. Fleming of Columbia, Tenn., won't talk about himself, but is happy to tell about the prowess of Curly. Master Sgt. Einar (Curly) Klabo of Kalispell, Mont., is the man to tell about John D., but not about himself. And they both talk about how good Goin' Jessie is.

Reason for Name

"Why do we call her Goin' Jessie? Well," drawled John D., "down where I come from, anythin' travels fast is known as a Goin' Jessie. See that picture of that rabbit up there on Goin' Jessie's nose? Well, that's a rabbit travelin' fast, known as the Goin' Jessie, too. See?"

Goin' Jessie, John D. and Curly will hasten to tell you, is the trip record-holder for the group.

"She," John D. beams, "has gone out on 33 missions so far without once havin' to turn back to the field for engine trouble of any kind. That's in four and a half months. That Curly. He's sure one good crew chief. Why, he's been a crew chief for five years, here and other places, and he's never had a plane go down on him, not one."

"Listen to that John D. talk," grinned Curly, emerging greasily from Goin' Jessie's engine.

"If there's success, it's always due to team work. John D.'s no slouch when it come to piloting a plane, either. He got a commendation from the general, he did. That was for the time one of his engines went out 200 miles from the target.

"He could have dropped his bombs in the ocean and not run into any danger of losing his neck by going in without an engine, he could have, but not John D. They'd told him to go after that certain target, and he was going to do it. He was out seven hours, he said afterward, and he said he figured after burning up that much gas he might just as well go on in and drop his bombs, and that's what he did."

One Jap Shot Down

Goin' Jessie has one Japanese fighter shot down and two damaged to her credit, Curly and John D. will race to tell you.

"I'm never in a bit of danger when I'm flyin'," John D. grinned, "because, you see, when the goin' gets tough, I just whistle 'Dixie' and I grab up the Confederate flag—the Stars and Bars, you know— which I keep hangin' right there handy in the cockpit, and I wave that flag and Goin' Jessie just settles right into it and we come through with flyin' colors."

But when John D. and the Goin' Jessie aren't back right on time, like the time John D. came in on the three engines, Curly's in a dither of a worry.

"He's always right out there to meet me," John D. grinned. And I'm always mighty glad to see ol' Curly there waitin'. So's Goin' Jessie. Curly starts right in to work on her, even if it's pourin' rain, or beatin' down sun and when he gets her ready to go out on the next mission, she's really ready."

That's the three-way team, John D., who was attending the University of Mississippi when the war broke out; Curly, the tall crew chief; and Goin' Jessie, a busy bombing B-29.

PACIFIC FRONT

Okinawa, July 7—This is a tour of the Okinawa battlefield after the guns have fallen silent—a battlefield where many valorous young Americans fell but carried with them into eternity an even greater number of Japanese.

The jeep bumps along—moving slowly through the dust clouds to keep from running down Okinawans—past the ruined and deserted villages into the rubble heap of what was once Naha, the capital of Okinawa.

Then up the hill to Shuri Castle, where the Japanese had their headquarters until the shells and bombs pulverized the walls, five feet thick.

Wreckage Tells Story

There was Chocolate Drop Hill, where the wreckage of 15 American tanks stopped by Japanese shells are mute monuments to the valor of the men who fell in the battle to conquer it.

It is peaceful now on Conical Hill, where the Americans fought up and were driven back and finally went up to stay.

Not far away is a cemetery where many of those who fought on Conical Hill lie buried. Helmeted soldiers are painting white crosses.

In the center of one cemetery was a low picket fence around the grave of Lieut. Gen. Simon Bolivar Buckner, Jr., commander of the U.S. Tenth Army, who fell just as final victory was in view.

The sporadic fire of Japanese snipers from distant Hill 89 reminds the visitor that men still are falling although the campaign has long since ended.

Japs Fight Fiercely

There is a cave, running two miles underground, containing a subterranean lake. The Japanese fought fiercely here.

Today a soldier pumped water from the lake for a shower bath.

On the way up to the mountains the roads are lined with the wreckage of Japanese equipment—planes, tanks, trucks and carts. And there are some American tanks and planes there too.

The Okinawa mountaineers are used to Americans now—but apparently not American women.

When we came upon them, they looked startled and seemed about to run away until one young woman mustered courage enough to come forward.

War Moves Away

She bowed to the ground, straightened up solemnly, threw both her hands over her head and waited. I waited too, and when nothing happened shook hands with her.

That broke the ice and she laughed and began jabbering away in Japanese. The others were reassured and gathered around to stare.

For the Okinawas too—once terrorized by the guns and bombs—the war now seemed far away.

NOTES

1. Bonnie Wiley, "First AP Woman Correspondent in the Pacific Relives Past Through Chance Encounter," AP Cleartime.
2. Ibid.
3. Ibid.
4. Bonnie Wiley, letter to author, 6 September 1986.
5. Ibid.
6. Ibid.
7. Bonnie Wiley, "Woman Writer in Plane Sees Desperate Battle on Okinawa."
8. Bonnie Wiley, letter to author, 19 July 1986.

7

Lyn Crost

"When the boys discovered I was going to stay on the front lines with them tonight, they found the best feather bed in the village and established a corner in the operations office where I could write." So wrote Lyn Crost, the war correspondent reporting to the *Honolulu Star-Bulletin* in 1945. "Just to make sure of my comfort, they found the best typewriter in the company and set it up on the only surface available, a sewing machine, and only regretted that there was no cushioned chair available to complete their handiwork."[1] The report was written while with the Seventh Army in Germany, but the focus of this report, as for most of the other reporting by Lyn Crost, was the men from the territory of Hawaii—men from the sugar cane and pineapple fields, postal workers, bus drivers, teachers, lawyers, who now fought for America's cause in World War II.

Lyn graduated from Brown University with many honors: Phi Beta Kappa, *magna cum laude*, Pembroke Scholar, University Scholar. Her career in journalism started while she was still a student. She worked part time on the *Providence Star-Tribune* which unfortunately went bankrupt four months before she graduated. She was offered a job with the other daily newspaper in Providence, Rhode Island, but since it was with the women's section, she wasn't interested. She sought a position in the newsroom, but this daily did not hire women for this type of reporting. She decided to go to Honolulu and try to get news reporting experience there. Her eventual plans included going on to the Orient where she thought she could find work with an English-language paper. Since she had a close relative who had lived in Hawaii from about the turn of the century and who invited Lyn to live with her, the plans seemed feasible.

In Honolulu she found work with Dr. James Shoemaker who was studying labor conditions in the territory for the U.S. Bureau of Labor

Lyn Crost. Photo courtesy of Lyn Crost.

Statistics. This served as a favorable background for Lyn, because she achieved a fundamental understanding of labor, industry, agricultural problems, and similar matters in the Territory of Hawaii. When that study was finished, she worked on a temporary basis for the *Honolulu Star-Bulletin*, covering a pan-Pacific medical convention, then as a substitute on the women's pages for someone on a long mainland vacation.

However, the *Honolulu Star-Bulletin* had a policy of not hiring women in the newsroom, so she found a job with the other Honolulu daily, *The Honolulu Advertiser*. The city editor of this newspaper was Robert Trumbull, who subsequently became a *New York Times* foreign correspondent and who wrote *The Raft*, an account of an incident in the Pacific during World War II.

Lyn worked at *The Honolulu Advertiser* for nearly two years, "doing everything and anything," as she says. This included news reporting, going offshore to meet ships coming in from the mainland or Orient, assisting in covering the territorial legislature, writing special features. "It was great experience."[2]

Then it became obvious that there would be war in the Pacific, and it would be inadvisable to go to the Orient, as Lyn had originally planned. In mid-1941 she returned to the mainland and found work in Washington, D.C., first in the Executive Office of the President with Dr. Pendleton Herring from Harvard. She assisted with a historical study that President Roosevelt had ordered regarding the war preparedness efforts of the United States. In the meantime, she kept in touch with newspaper friends and when there was an opening for covering news with the Associated Press bureau, she was hired. Most of her reporting was from the congressional offices.

In late 1944 the *Honolulu Star-Bulletin* asked if Lyn would be interested in being its European war correspondent. The publisher of this newspaper was Joseph R. Farrington. He was the only American publisher who thought enough of what the Nisei (persons of Japanese descent but born in the United States and loyal to it) were doing in Europe to send a reporter there to cover their story.

The Nisei were already serving in the U.S. Army by the time Pearl Harbor was attacked. In early 1942 Japanese-American men of draft age were classified as 4-C, enemy aliens. Those already drafted in the army were retained. It wasn't until two years later that they no longer classified the Nisei as 4-C, but treated them like other American citizens, which was all the Nisei wanted.

When, in 1943, the Department of War announced plans to form a

Japanese-American combat unit, it intended to induct 1,500 volunteers from Hawaii, but almost 10,000 volunteers showed up. The Nisei served with distinction. During the attack on Monte Cassino, they earned the sobriquet "Purple Heart battalion" because of their great losses and intrepid stand. When the battalion entered Italy at Salerno, it numbered 1,300 men. After Monte Cassino its effectives totaled 521.

The men of the 100th Infantry Battalion, who were Japanese-Americans except for a few Caucasian officers, were all from Hawaii. This was the first Japanese-American outfit to see battlefield action. By the time Lyn arrived in Europe, another Japanese-American outfit, the 442nd Infantry Combat Team, was also there and included men from Hawaii as well as the mainland. The two outfits were joined and became the 100th/442nd Regimental Combat Team. They were to become the most highly decorated military unit for its size and length of service in U.S. history. Lyn learned that captured German documents revealed that Germans reinforced their troops whenever the Nisei were on the line. They feared them and called them the "Terrible Turks." "Axis Sally," in her broadcasts from Rome, referred to the Nisei as "America's secret weapon." She played Hawaiian music for them and urged them to go home and enjoy themselves on their beautiful beaches.

The Nisei were well disciplined. There were no cases of AWOL among them, except "reverse AWOLS" when they left hospitals before being officially dismissed because they wanted to get back on the line with their units. They were a closely knit group, always watching out for each other's welfare.

Lyn resigned from AP and accepted the assignment with the *Honolulu Star-Bulletin*. She reported mostly from Italy, sometimes from Germany, and occasionally from France, but her primary interest was to report on anybody who came from Hawaii, or on any events that would be of particular interest in Hawaii. She wrote human interest stories and other stories with a Hawaii angle; the wire services carried stories about major troop movements so she did not concentrate on these.

In a dispatch printed on April 19, 1945, in the *Honolulu Star-Bulletin*, Lyn wrote about the highly praised Hawaii troops. Gen. Alexander M. Patch, commander of the Seventh Army in Germany, called them "among the very best fighters in the American army."[3] The mere mention of these boys, Lyn said, brought immediate praise. Generals Patch and Ralph C. Tobin (who commanded the Hawaii boys in France) had many examples to relate about a unit that they could be proud of. The only trouble, they said, was finding winter clothes to fit them and extra rice rations. General Tobin managed to get them a 10 percent increase in rice rations, but disagreed with them on the best way to eat it. The problem of clothing to fit the regiment was more serious, but finally experts in army salvage and the quartermaster corps found shoes and parkas that were small enough.

Lyn reported one of General Tobin's favorite stories about a Hawaii boy he was decorating with the Distinguished Service Cross and the Silver Star. "Despite his fearlessness on the front lines, the boy shook like a leaf during the presentation until General Tobin told him to be thankful the French were not awarding the decoration because they would insist on kissing him."[4]

On another occasion she wrote a feature article from Italy about a "tired, unshaved and wrinkled man who shouldn't be in the front lines."[5] This was Doc Kometani (Capt. Katsumi Kometani) for whom the soldiers were more than dog-tag numbers; they were kids he'd watched grow up. She told of how he walked through impossible and dangerous terrain to be with the wounded men who needed medical assistance. This former Honolulu dentist, forty years old at the time, wa seen as a "chief morale booster" and one of the most highly respected men in the regiment. "The boys look on Capt. Kometani as the father of this Purple Heart battalion."[6]

One of Lyn's articles had the headline "Islanders Can Take It." She quoted Maj. Alex McKenzie, the only *haole* (Caucasian) officer with the original 100th Infantry Battalion, who said the following about the men in his regiment: "They have tremendous physical endurance. . . . And they just never retreated. Why I don't know. If they had to take a licking they just sat and took it. It tore my heart out just to watch them."[7] But, he added, they could "dish it out" too. He said that the men in his battalion stuck together. "Everybody tries to help everybody else. They're easy kids to work and live with . . . and as any soldier who has ever fought with them will vouch, they're tops in combat."[8]

Lyn wrote about Shorty, possibly the shortest soldier in the army. Private First Class Takeshi Kumura was only four feet nine inches tall. The army, Lyn said, wanted nothing to do with him, but somehow he got himself accepted, "and now the army wouldn't think of trying to get rid of him."[9] Shorty received a Purple Heart while with the 442nd Regiment in Italy.

Some of Lyn's stories told of the humorous side to the war. One of these, written while with the 442nd Regiment in Italy, began like this:

"If you're ever tempted to sock a mule in the jaw then read this."[10] She told of how the Hawaii boys tried to work with mules, and the stubbornness they encountered—a common trait in mules. Anse Arakaki tried to make Big Red move by a swift right uppercut to the mule's jaw, but ended up being hospitalized himself with a fractured wrist.

Other stories she wrote were, for example, from England, where a former territorial attorney general was stationed with the War Crimes Commission. From Heidelberg, Germany, she wrote a long story on military government in that town, comparing it with some aspects of the Hawaii military government after the bombing of Pearl Harbor.

Lyn was one of the first American correspondents at Buchenwald and she was horrified to see human bones in a heap and smell the stench of burned human flesh. Her poignant account of talking with the survivors appeared in the *Star-Bulletin* in April 1945. She wrote, "The French are burying here today [April 12] the last of approximately 18,000 Jews who died from beating, execution and disease in the latest Nazi concentration camp discovered by advancing Allied armies."[11]

The troops on whom she reported certainly didn't have any bias against women reporters. "The troops were so happy to see reporters that they would have helped any of them in any way possible, man or woman. In that way I don't think I had any special advantages," Lyn said.[12]

She wrote on April 20, 1945, while with the Seventh Army in Germany, about the takeover of a new village. "The front progresses so fast here that sometimes they move every day. . . . We moved in [a German village] during the late afternoon and watched the island boys clear the barns and houses and establish a mess and sleeping quarters while worried Germans looked on."[13] The Hawaii troops also found places to keep their stray pets, everything from pheasants to dogs, that they had picked up in Italy, France, and Germany. She located a gun crew in a clearing beside a farmhouse, "with Technician Fifth Grade Tetsuo Tomita of Maui helping to prepare captured German macaroni, beets, string beans and pineapple for the midday meal. His only complaint is that he can't get enough rice. It had been three weeks since he has had rice."[14] She added that the officers had many tales to tell about the boys' bravery and humor. Officers particularly enjoyed relating how the islanders, instead of talking code over the communications, talked a mixture of Japanese, Hawaiian, Filipino, and Chinese which, they said, was "ironclad" against enemy deduction.

In Germany and Italy she stayed as close as possible to the Japanese-

American troops. The record of these Japanese-Americans during the war was a terrific inspiration to her, particularly when she realized that many of those men from the mainland had left families behind them in concentration camps. They experienced a paradoxical tragedy— frontline fighting to defend the United States and worry about the welfare of their families incarcerated behind barbed wire and under armed guard in the ten concentration camps established by the U.S. government. Yet she could also write, "Islanders Strum Ukes; Songs of Hawaii Are Filling the Air of Italy." The article said, "If Italy doesn't know its Hawaiian music by the time this regiment gets ready to move out, it's no fault of the island boys."[15]

The 522nd Field Artillery Battalion had the unique experience of coming across some Dachau prisoners who had been taken from the prison camp a week before the Nazis knew the Americans were coming. These prisoners were forced to march over the Bavarian mountains. Of the eight thousand who started the march, only five thousand survived. "This meeting was indelibly imprinted on the minds of many island boys."[16]

Lyn wrote the first story ever carried in any newspaper about a Nisei hero, Lt. Daniel K. Inouye of Honolulu. He won the Distinguished Service Cross for extraordinary heroism during a battle in the Po Valley campaign. He was wounded when a hand grenade shattered his right arm, but he continued to direct his platoon. Inouye went on to have a distinguished career as senator from Hawaii.[17]

Lyn's working and living conditions varied greatly. She stayed in the big hotels in London (the Cumberland), in Paris (the Scribe, which had been commandeered by the U.S. Army), and in Rome (the Hassler, run by the British army). In Germany she lived with the 522nd Field Artillery Battalion, moving with them from place to place, sleeping in houses, some bombed-out, some intact. Her desk might have been something like an old kitchen table, a sewing machine, her lap. In Italy she lived in a series of tents in a very muddy field. Another time it was on the grounds of a villa where she had a trailer all to herself, complete with all amenities.

Her Japanese-American friends were solicitous about her welfare, and always inquired about facilities for her. When they were stationed in one spot long enough to set up shower facilities, they would clear out the shower area, station a guard around it, and allow Lyn the privilege of a good, long shower in perfect comfort. "Obviously," she said, "no male reporter would have gotten such good service."[18]

Lyn became the first and only woman member of the famed 442nd

Veterans Club in 1946, a singular honor from the men about whom she wrote so descriptively and compassionately.

When the war ended, Lyn worked as the Washington correspondent for the *Honolulu Star-Bulletin* for a year. After that she married and worked as a special assistant in the White House during Eisenhower's first term for three years. Since that time she has not been active in the field of journalism.

Lyn Crost, who was billed as the "*Star-Bulletin* War Correspondent who is reporting to this newspaper from the battlefront in Europe," served credibly along with her peers. She recalls that the AP personnel were always most helpful, and the few times she had to share a jeep with any male reporters they were always respectful and helpful. "If you are a professional reporter, you are a reporter and that's all there is to it."[19]

In October of 1987 a special Smithsonian Institution exhibit opened. "A More Perfect Union," as the exhibit was called, focused on the Japanese-American experience during World War II. At that time Lyn was honored for bringing the story of the Nisei to the American public. A sign in the Smithsonian says, "Lyn Crost, a war correspondent for the *Honolulu Star-Bulletin*, took a special interest in the men of the 100th/442nd. Her dispatches from the front, and those of other war correspondents, underscored the courage and sacrifice of the men who fought for their nation while family and friends remained behind barbed wire."[20]

A SAMPLE OF WAR REPORTING BY LYN CROST

GEN. CLARK STRONG IN PRAISE OF HAWAII TROOPS OF 442ND

Monday, April 30, 1945. With the 5th Army group in Italy, April 30—The 442nd Infantry Regiment, composed of Japanese-American troops from Hawaii, entered Turin, the important center of heavy industry in northern Italy, early today following a swift advance up the western coast.

News of the entry reached Gen. Mark W. Clark, U.S. 5th Army commander, as I interviewed him this afternoon at his headquarters there.

We had been discussing the record of the 442nd, which Gen. Clark told me has done "one of the most magnificent jobs of this war," when his aide informed him of the liberation of Turin.

Gen. Clark smiled, then turned and said: "They are in Turin now."

Earlier, Gen. Clark, in response to press inquiries, had said:

"The military power of Germany in Italy has practically ceased even though scattered fighting may continue as remnants of the German armies are mopped up."

Troops of this army group, he said, had so smashed the German armies in Italy that they have been "virtually eliminated as a military force."

The 442nd Regiment's role in this offensive has been to spearhead much of the drive up the coast, which last week resulted in the fall of Genoa, the second largest seaport on the Mediterranean, which is important in supplying the entire northern section of Italy.

Gen. Clark told me he made a special visit to greet troops of the 442nd when they returned to this theater after hard fighting in the Vosges mountains and the French maritime Alps.

The troops, of which the Hawaii boys form a large part, have fought with Gen. Clark throughout the drive up Italy from the first perilous landings in the southern section.

"They are wonderful fighters," Gen. Clark told me, as he traced their progress on a map in the briefing room.

He said he was particularly thankful to have them in the present fighting in northern Italy because of their record for mountain fighting.

Although the regiment's progress up the coast has been swift, it has met heavy resistance from crack German troops, particularly in the area north of Massa, as it was en route to capture the great naval base of La Spezia, which fell to it last week.

The feeling is marked here today that the end to the Italian campaign may come at any moment. The destruction of the German armies in this sector has been accomplished in an offensive now 22 days old for the 8th army and 15 days old for the 5th army. In his formal statement on the situation, Gen. Clark announced:

"Twenty five German divisions, some of the best in the German army, have been torn to pieces and can no longer effectively resist our armies. Thousands of vehicles, tremendous quantities of arms and equipment and over 120,000 prisoners have been captured, and many more are being corralled."

NOTES

1. Lyn Crost, "Moving Fast, Taking Town, All in a Day's Work for Hawaii Soldiers," *Honolulu Star-Bulletin*, 20 April 1945.

2. Lyn Crost, letter to author, 28 September 1986.

3. Lyn Crost, "Patch Names Hawaii Soldiers As 'Among Best in American Army,'" *Honolulu Star-Bulletin*, 19 April 1945.

4. Ibid.

5. Lyn Crost, "Doc Kometani Spells Home to Boys of 100th Regiment," *Honolulu Star-Bulletin*, 19 May 1945.

6. Ibid.

7. Lyn Crost, "Islanders Can Take It," *Honolulu Star-Bulletin*, n.d.

8. Ibid.

9. Lyn Crost, "A Story About Shorty," *Honolulu Star-Bulletin*, n.d.

10. Lyn Crost, "Handling Mules," *Honolulu Star-Bulletin*, n.d.

11. Lyn Crost, "French Bury Last of 18,000 Jews Slain in Nazi Concentration Camp," *Honolulu Star-Bulletin*, 16 April 1945.

12. Crost, letter.

13. Crost, "Moving Fast."

14. Ibid.

15. Lyn Crost, "Islanders Strum Ukes," *Honolulu Star-Bulletin*, 11 June 1945.

16. Lyn Crost, "Islanders At Dachau," *Honolulu Star-Bulletin*, 3 July 1945.

17. Lyn Crost, "Daniel K. Inouye Wins DSC In Action In Italy," *Honolulu Star-Bulletin*, 26 October 1945.

18. Crost, letter.

19. Ibid.

20. Chris Collins, "Star-Bulletin Reporter Brought the War Home," *Honolulu Star-Bulletin*, 1 October 1987.

8

Helen Kirkpatrick

"Helen Kirkpatrick has earned her position as America's foremost woman war correspondent through her dispatches pounded out at white heat while the blitz surged about and above her in London bomb shelters, in Coventry, on Dover's white cliffs." So read a wartime information sheet about the London correspondent for the *Chicago Daily News*. "Clear as crystal, accurate as a radio beam, prompt as the crashing impact of the happenings they record, her cablegrams have literally been filed at machine gun tempo—often as many as three, four and even five a day."

Helen Kirkpatrick and Mary Welsh were the first two women who went through the process and received both their accreditation and uniforms as war correspondents. According to Lael Wertenbaker, who knew Helen in London, "She was somebody that everyone trusted. She had the best sources in the business. She wrote factually and was a very good correspondent."

Helen was born in 1909 in Rochester, New York. She received her B.A. from Smith College in 1931, graduating *cum laude* and as a Phi Beta Kappa. She then did graduate work at the University of Geneva in Switzerland, studying international law. When she returned to the United States, the depression had hit the country in full force and she discovered nobody wanted to give a job to someone who could speak French and understood international law—but could do little else. She finally found a job as a reporter for the *New York Herald Tribune* for $15 a week, but with it came the warning from the city editor that there was no future for women in the world of journalism.

The warning had its impact, and Helen found work at Macy's department store and shortly after that she married. When that marriage ended in divorce in 1935, Helen decided to return to Geneva. She worked for the Foreign Policy Association, writing for its publica-

Helen Kirkpatrick. Photo courtesy of Helen Kirkpatrick.

tion, and occasionally for the *New York Herald Tribune* as well as for British newsmen when they had to be out of town. While with the Foreign Policy Association she often met foreign correspondents, and this eventually led to a regular job with the *Chicago Daily News* in 1939. In the meantime Helen had moved to London in 1937 and instituted the *Whitehall Letter*, an informative publication of world news that became widely respected and read by world leaders such as Winston Churchill. In this newsletter she warned of an impending war and that Hitler would attempt a takeover of the world. Also during this time Helen wrote two books, *This Terrible Peace* in 1938, and *Under the British Umbrella* in 1939.

When she joined the *Chicago Daily News*, she became "the only woman on that paper's large, crack foreign staff and one of the few American women correspondents then filing from Europe."[1] She requested, as her first assignment, permission to write about the former Edward VIII of England, by then the Duke of Windsor. Her colleagues derided her ambition, since the duke gave no interviews. Helen persisted and by contacting people with whom the duke was staying she reached him. Her first story for the *Chicago Daily News* was this rare interview that had eluded her peers.

She covered many important and critical areas: Prague, Spain, the Balkans, Poland, Italy, Germany, France, and Algiers. Before long she achieved a reputation for being a shrewd analyst of world affairs and for inside stories on international events. "Eight days before the blitzkrieg in the west she cabled exclusive information that the King of Belgium had advised the American government that his country expected to be the next victim of the Nazis."[2]

After the defeat of France, she reported on French ships arriving in Britain, but did so through cryptic messages designed to circumvent the censors. She wrote items such as " 'Marianne Gobs arrived safely with many of her possessions.' "[3] Later, however, she came to the conclusion that censorship was more significant than just an effort to frustrate reporters, so she stopped trying to sneak messages to the *Daily News*.

During the blitz attacks on London, Helen rode with fire engines and ambulances and reported on the devastation she witnessed. During this time, Edward R. Murrow wanted to hire Helen. "Kirkpatrick's voice was low-pitched and decisive; more important, she was one of the best correspondents in London."[4] CBS denied the request—no more women. Murrow hired Charles Collingwood, "a young UP correspondent ... with only a year's experience and nothing like Kirkpatrick's stature, but more acceptable to New York."5

Helen also wrote from Ireland, covering the arrival of the Second American Expeditionary Force, and reported from the North Sea and eastern Atlantic from on board warships. She followed the invading army into Normandy and became one of the first journalists to enter liberated Paris. "There she scored an eyewitness scoop on the attempted assassination of French Gen. DeGaulle in a cathedral."6 While in Paris she assumed the position of bureau chief of the *Daily News*.

When Helen first became a war correspondent in 1942, she and Mary Welsh who was with *Time* magazine were the first women accredited to cover the Allied armies. Being accredited meant having to wear a uniform, but since the WACs had not been organized yet, no one knew what kind of uniform the two women should wear. Helen and Mary went to a British tailor and requested uniforms just like the men's, only with skirts instead of pants. Later the WACs wore uniforms very similar to those designed by that British tailor.

In 1946 Helen resigned from the *Daily News* and became roving European correspondent for the *New York Post*. From 1949–1951 she worked in Paris as chief of the information division of the Economical Cooperation Administration. Her work contributed to the successful implementation of the Marshall Plan, an ambitious plan for rehabilitating Europe. She then became a public affairs advisor in 1951 for the Department of State, Bureau of European Affairs. A newspaper article reported that "because of the many years she lived in Europe, . . . Miss Kirkpatrick is ideally equipped to make contacts with newsmen in Europe, to advise Secretary [of State Dean] Acheson and his delegation on the press and public opinion in that part of Europe."7 Finally, Helen served as assistant to the president of Smith College from 1953–1955. She married Robbins Milbank in 1954.

When Helen received a citation from her alma mater, The Masters School in Dobbs Ferry, New York, the president of the alumnae association read the same text as the president of Smith College had when Helen received an honorary M.A. in 1948. "A graduate with honors from Smith College, you have won still greater honors far from Northampton. As staff member of the office of the Foreign Policy Association in Geneva, as London correspondent of the *Chicago Daily News*, and as war correspondent with the American Expeditionary Force during the late conflict. . . . A profound analyst of world affairs, a writer of distinction, an ambassador of Democracy and of the dignity and worth of man, wherever he may live, and a courageous champion of all things just and true, you have conferred honors upon your college and your country."

SAMPLE OF WAR REPORTING BY HELEN KIRKPATRICK

WHAT THE SOLDIERS THINK

Allied Headquarters, Algiers, Oct. 27—If most of the U.S. is swinging away from isolationism the same cannot be said of the rank and file of the Army. Responsibility for this difference in outlook must be placed square-ly at the door of the Army and its Special Services, in the view of this correspondent and a good many thinking soldiers to whom I have talked.

Having seen North Africa, for example, without benefit of explana-tion, the average soldier is going to be likely to say at home: "I know Algeria. Let me explain the Arab-Jewish problem. Hand Algeria back to the Arabs," or some other equally misinformed, superficial opinion wrung from him by admiring friends.

Listening to officers who too often are themselves haters of foreign-ers, he is getting the idea that the best thing Americans can do is stay at home and mind their own business.

"All we do is to hand out stuff to these people and they don't know how to use it, or they fight among themselves"—such may be the verdict of the average man. And that may become a second American if not world tragedy, which could be easily avoided if certain steps were taken now.

There are so many examples of what happens to the average American who arrives in, say Algeria, that it is difficult to choose anyone in particular. One day a few weeks ago, a red-haired GI was drowsing in front of the press building when the usual type of over-loaded Arab wagon passed by and the overburdened horse slipped on the cobblestones.

The Arab driver beat the horse severely. The red-headed American leaped from his jeep and administered a severe beating to the Arab. City Arabs' treatment of horses is a subject of extreme criticism from U.S. soldiers who are equally critical, and often illogically so, of French treatment of Arabs.

At the same time, there is co-operation here among Americans and British such as has never been seen before in history between two allies. And in the field there is the same mutual respect and liking. In the back areas, however, Americans and British have separate camps and the only contact the men may have there is in cafes and on the street.

Obviously there is need for Army education, which means education and not fifth-rate entertainment. Books, speakers and discussion groups in the Army could do much to orient the American soldier without giving him a biased or slanted viewpoint.

Soldiers are hungry for facts—facts on what Fascism really did in Italy and how it came to fall; what the characteristics of various European countries are, and why things have happened as they have during the last 20 years.

The more thoughtful young officers and men will sit around for hours telling you how pernicious they believe is the influence of Hollywood and certain types of radio programs and newspapers which pander to the lowest rather than to the highest level of reader intelligence, and it is hard to escape the impression here that the Army is following faithfully in the footsteps of Hollywood, the radio and those newspapers in that respect.

The cause is not hard to ascertain—it seems to be fear of political controversy and its repercussions in the U.S. But a group of 50 soldiers discussing this the other night said in effect: "The British have two political parties, but their soldiers seem able to get reading matter on controversial subjects presented to them. Why can't we?"

NOTES

1. Isabelle Shelton, "Takes Off for Europe at the Drop of a Hat," *Washington Star*, 7 August 1952.

2. Marion Marzolf, *Up from the Footnote* (New York: Hastings House, 1977), 70.

3. Shelton, "Takes Off for Europe."

4. A.M. Sperber, *Murrow: His Life and Times* (New York: Freundlich Books, 1986), 177.

5. Ibid.

6. Shelton, "Takes Off for Europe."

7. Ibid.

9

Catherine Coyne

When Catherine Coyne returned from her stint as a war correspondent during World War II, she said she had already had her "dream assignment." "The war experience was one I wouldn't have missed for anything," she recalled. "There were times when I was cold and hungry, but something happened later to make everything seem perfect."[1]

Catherine Coyne first became interested in journalism while in high school as she worked on the school magazine and yearbook. She attended Boston University because it had a journalism program, and graduated with the class of 1930. Because of the depression she was unable to find a job on a daily newspaper so she worked for a trade magazine devoted to the interests of monument dealers. After it folded, she went to work for the *Boston Herald* and as a stringer for a New York financial paper, *Time*, *Life*, *Fortune*, and *Architectural Forum*. For the *Herald* she did feature writing and general assignments. She had the distinction of being the only female on the city staff.

Then, rather unexpectedly, her boss, George Minot, the managing editor of the *Herald*, asked if Catherine would like to cover some of the war overseas for a month or two. At first the Pacific was suggested, but when the *Herald* personnel decided she'd be lost out there, the assignment was changed to Europe. Catherine was anxious to go. "Mr. Minot's assignment to me was a dream. It was to write anything interesting."[2]

Catherine set out, not the least bit apprehensive once she boarded the ship. "There were four USO girls, me and five thousand troops," she recalled.[3] She landed in Liverpool and found herself on her own. She obtained some English money, then found a room to rent in the attic of a house that had a fish market on the ground floor and mice in the walls. That first night she pulled a blanket over her head as she

Catherine Coyne. Photo courtesy of Catherine Coyne.

heard the mice scurrying around; then the absurdity of the situation struck her. She thought, "I'm afraid of a mouse, and a plane could come over at any minute."[4]

The next morning Catherine went to press headquarters and there met Lieutenant Commander Joseph Mutrie who in civilian life was on the staff of the *Boston Globe*, Chief Petty Officer Nathaniel H. Sperber, and Seaman Gerry McCann, all with the U.S. Coast Guard. Sperber was also on the staff of *The Boston Traveler* and his wife worked for the *Herald*. These people "more or less became my 'mother hens,' " Catherine said. Although Catherine was accredited to the army and had the courtesy rank of captain, she wrote a great deal about the men of the coast guard who were experts with small boats and thus important to the invasion, especially for search and rescue. "I had absolutely free rein to write anything that interested me. We wrote about the civilians and what they were doing. . . . I wrote about the soldiers—about interesting boys from the New England area."[5] During her time in London she wrote about buzz bombs (she received a special bonus for one of these stories) and the pubs that were here today and gone tomorrow.

Catherine eventually found a room at the Mount Royal Hotel with the help of a woman at the British Ministry. This became a much more comfortable "home," particularly since the building looked indestructible.

Then came D-Day, and at three o'clock in the morning Catherine received a telephone call that she should go to the British Ministry of Information. There she met Marjorie Avery of the *Detroit Free Press*, who thoughtfully ordered coffee and toast for her. "Thus began a very warm friendship," Catherine said.[6] They learned about the invasion during that early-morning meeting and then Catherine went to the south of England to interview the wounded from Normandy at the military hospitals.

Following this she was invited to be with the WACs when they were sent to France. She discovered there was much to do in preparation for living in a tent. Nat Sperber, who had a way with supply sergeants, was able to get not just two but six blankets for her bedroll and extra covers for "my smelly gas outfit," which she used as a pillow. It was never opened, she recalled.

Her stalwart friends assured her she would get sick during the crossing of the Channel because "everybody did." They counseled her to find her bunk as soon as she got on the troop ship, crawl into it, wrap up in a blanket, and swallow a seasickness pill. Catherine boarded around five o'clock in the morning and did as she was told. She felt she had just dozed off when she heard much racket and woke to find Marjorie Avery shaking her and calling her name. "It was difficult to find my tongue but I croaked, 'Is this a practice alert or the real thing?' She giggled and said, 'Neither. It's lunch.' It was noon and we were still at the dock, still loading. It was a pleasant crossing."[7]

As the ship anchored off Omaha Beach she watched the soldiers gingerly climb down from the ship via a cargo net hung over the side of the ship. Being afraid of heights, she watched them with increasing dismay, all the time trying to work up the courage to follow, although she felt she would never leave the ship. When all the men had left the ship, the women's turn came. "The military, in its strange wisdom, put down a gangplank—a flight of stairs—down which we went to a small craft."[8]

Catherine and the others were billeted in tents in "a very smelly apple orchard." As they prepared for the night, Dudley Ann Harmon, a correspondent for United Press, complained she only had the tarp shell of her bedroll because she had felt sorry for her bombed-out friends in London and had given them her blankets. Catherine donated one of hers to Dudley Ann.

Catherine recalled that she had quite a ritual in getting ready for sleep. She tucked her long hair into the knitted liner of her helmet, put on pajamas over her underwear, put a folded sweater into the tops of her pajama bottoms, put on the lining of her raincoat, then crawled in along with her boots. During the first night she had left her boots on the ground by her cot, but found snails in them in the morning. After that they joined her under the covers. She recalled that it was cold and damp at night but they managed to stay healthy.

In Normandy she and Virginia Irwin met Joshua Logan, a theatrical director whom Catherine had met and interviewed in Boston. He was now a press officer for an air force fighter group, and he wanted Catherine and Virginia to write a story about his group. Virginia refused; she felt the air force had had plenty of publicity and now was the time for the foot soldier. Joshua offered various inducements, but couldn't convince the women. Finally he said, "If you girls will come I'll see that you get a nice warm shower bath."[9] That did it, Catherine recalled. They went behind a fence, and pulled a rope that brought sun-warmed water down on them from a suspended barrel. This was a welcome change, especially since they had been subjected to washing with cold water in their helmets.

When Catherine got to Paris, she became acquainted with Lee

Miller who was accredited as a photographer for *Vogue* magazine. She arranged for Catherine to meet Pablo Picasso, who took them to lunch with friends of his.

In Paris Catherine began to feel the "war was getting away from us." Women, she recalled, had special difficulty in securing transportation, and even though gossip and rumor abounded, there was less and less to write about. Then one of the press officers arranged occasional trips to the front for small groups of correspondents. During one of these, Catherine and Marjorie stayed at the Ninth Air Force press camp, located in a small, charming hotel normally a favorite with the diplomatic corps in peacetime. This became their home base for some time, and they were, in effect, with the Third Army. From here they covered stories in Holland, Belgium, Luxembourg, France, and Germany. They hitched rides by jeep and plane, from the British as well as the Americans.

Catherine and Marjorie Avery covered one of Gen. George Patton's press conferences in Luxembourg. "Patton didn't like having women around, but Dot [Marjorie] and I were in the front row." Patton never used the phrase "the enemy," but chose to say "the son of a bitch." After each utterance he would look at the women and apologize.[10]

In April 1945 Catherine and Marjorie were at Leipzig and headed for Torgau. At that point they had a driver who was so bad that Catherine ended up doing most of the driving. They went down to the Elbe and looked across to where the Russians were. A man offered to take them across in a racing shell. She recalled that he all but "talked" it across the river. Once with the Russians, "we ate a lot of chocolate and drank eau de vie, which I didn't like. . . . We went up on a patio and danced."[11] Catherine was "picked up" by a Russian captain who pinned a red star on her jacket. While dancing, she was photographed by a newsreel crew, and the scene was used much later in a film starring Alec Guinness, *The Last Ten Days of Hitler*. Catherine remembered that nobody really understood each other during that celebration on the banks of the Elbe, but language didn't present much of a barrier.

Catherine wrote her impressions about this event: "These past few days have been too hilariously hectic for objective, reasoned thinking. Emotions were assaulted by events so unreal in their mixture of drama, tragedy and merry comedy. . . . We saw historic drama in the linking of two great armies to divide Germany."[12] She further commented on the drama of watching the German nation disintegrate, the happy ending to the tragedy of half-starved, tortured prisoners, and the excitement of the fraternization of Russian and American soldiers.

She said the German nation was so badly beaten that "a timid woman like this correspondent could ride unafraid through uncaptured German towns and wooded areas, past fully armed German soldiers who snivelingly pleaded with her to accept their surrender before Russians got them."[13]

After the war Catherine covered the Nuremberg war criminal trials, then flew home "with a headful of memories and a new hairdo."[14] She was asked to become city editor of the *Herald*, but she refused. She felt she had already had her "dream assignment." Instead she became chief of the bureau at the State House and wrote a Sunday political column. In 1948 she resigned to marry Judge Eugene A. Hudson of the Massachusetts Superior Court.

SAMPLE OF WAR REPORTING BY CATHERINE COYNE

AMERICANS AND RUSSIANS JOIN FORCES AT THE ELBE
(FROM *THE BOSTON HERALD*)

TORGAU, Germany, April 27—Americans and Russians in their historic long-awaited link-up in their joint war against Germany provided the world with a hilarious preview of VE-Day in a sunny meadow on the bank of the Elbe river here this afternoon.

There was a ceremony, of course. Maj.-Gen. E.F. Reinhardt, commanding general of the 69th Infantry Division, one of whose second lieutenants made the first contact unofficially and accidentally late yesterday afternoon, crossed the Elbe in a rowboat to meet a major general of the 58th Guards Division of the Red Army.

They shook hands, posed for thousands of pictures in the center of a screaming, shoving mob of official professional and amateur cameramen, then feasted in a German barracks on captured German eggs, black bread with cheese and tumblers of champagne and eau de vivre, an inferior cognac bottled for the Wehrmacht.

Primarily, however, it was a day for the little man of the armies—for the GI and the junior officer—and each made it a merry one, forgetting war while toasting the United States and Russia, swapping insignia and watches, snapping pictures and trying out one another's weapons amid noise, danger and laughter reminiscent of the Fourth of July at home.

Even the first contact with our ally was made without knowledge and consent of army brass. As a matter of fact, the first official reaction when 2nd Lt. William D. Robertson of Los Angeles and three enlisted men including Cpl. James J. McDonnell of Peabody brought a Russian liaison party back to battalion headquarters with them last night was a curt "By what authority did you make that contact?"

But just as today was merry so last night was one of excitement when unofficial acts could be forgiven. Germans crowding around battalion headquarters were thrown into near panic by the sight of three Russian officers, and an enlisted man—a suspected Gestapo agent—put his chin on a soldier's automatic rifle, pulled the trigger and shot his face off. Neither Americans nor Russians were moved.

Maj. Victor G. Conley of 120 Church Street, West Roxbury, First Battalion commander, was the first senior American officer to greet the Russians. He gave them champagne, posed with them for snapshots taken by soldiers like Staff Sgt. Walter F. Reardon, of Charlestown, who readily agreed to give each of them prints. Then the guests were whisked off by armed jeeps to division headquarters where arrangements were completed for today's meeting.

Long before the hour of the meeting, however, Yanks were at the river bank with a big sign reading "East meets West, Courtesy 69th Division." It depicted a Yank shaking hands with a Red soldier with buildings of New York and Moscow forming the background. Russians swarmed across the river in captured seven-oared racing shells.

They strolled the deserted town with Americans, every now and then to practice each other's words and each other's pistols. Military insignia was curiously mixed, and many a boy from a staunchly conservative American family today proudly wore the Red Star with crossed hammer and sickle of Communism.

A Russian captain early this afternoon took me by the arm, pointed across the Elbe and then at me. "See Russians?" he asked. I nodded vigorously. He led me to one of the frail racing shells which somehow, with two oars and much shouting, got us to the other side. He pinned the brass star from his cap on my jacket, led me along a cobbled tree-shaded path to a German barracks where I was offered a strange assortment of impossible drinks and black bread. There was a solemn toast to the memory of Roosevelt, a rousing cheer for Truman and an order for bottoms-up in honor of Stalin.

In our group were a woman correspondent from Detroit, Lt. Joseph J. Kovarik of New York, three captains from Siberia and a lieutenant from the Ukraine. They sang Russian songs then demanded of us an American tune. We gave them "Birmingham Jail," a sweetly sad song the 17th Airborne soldiers sang as they flew to jump east of the Rhine.

Nearly every Russian manning light guns in the fortress enclosure had a musical instrument, a harmonica, an accordion or a mandolin so that the air was filled with a mixture of tunes mingled with laughter and shouts of "Tovarich," which seemed to be the principal verbal link between Yank and Russian.

At one point a friend and I were grabbed by two Russian GI's prompted by a Red major to dance on the cobbled walk between the guns while amateur photographers went to work and Russian girl soldiers and nurses came to cheer us. It was difficult to determine whether laughter or the difficult steps exhausted us most.

A surprising aspect of the meeting was the similarity of Russian and American GI's. They seemed to have the same instincts. The interests were identical and they were like small boys when they gathered in little groups to break down their automatic rifles into their component parts and test the sights. They collected the same type of souvenirs— German knives, Luger pistols, Leica cameras, binoculars and insignia.

It was a day of laughter. Boys laughed when they danced Russian and hillbilly dances. They laughed when they crossed the river in the frail craft, they laughed as they skirted mines on our side of the Elbe and they laughed jeeringly when they passed Germans on the road— Germans like the officer in a horse-drawn carriage who frantically waved a white rag at me begging to be taken captive before the Russians caught up with him, and they laughed almost tearfully when they met half-starved Americans escaped from prisoner of war camps like Pfc. Frank Bartz of Stevens Point, Wisc., machine gunner with Seventh Armored Division captured in the December break-through, as he crawled into my jeep. Bartz struggled to keep back his tears when he asked between laughter and sobs: "Say, is this war over or has everybody just gone crazy?"

NOTES

1. Catherine Coyne Hudson, letter to author, 4 April 1987.
2. Ibid.
3. Marcia J. Monbleau, "World War II Link-Up in Germany Forty Years Ago This Week," *The Cape Codder*, 23 April 1985, p. 4.
4. Ibid.
5. Ibid.
6. Hudson, letter.
7. Ibid.
8. Ibid.
9. Ibid.
10. Monbleau, "Forty Years Ago."
11. Ibid.

12. Catherine Coyne, "Soldiers More Alike Than Not, Says War Correspondent Coyne," 29 April 1945, reprinted in *The Cape Codder*, 23 April 1985, p. 5.

13. Ibid.

14. Monbleau, "Forty Years Ago."

10

Alice-Leone Moats

"The reason my book, *Blind Date With Mars*, was a best seller was because I told the truth!" So stated Alice-Leone Moats when commenting on her experiences as a war correspondent in Russia, Iran, Egypt, and Africa. "I was the first one to tell it like it was in Russia—for example, that there were eighteen million political prisoners in Russia."

Following this eighteen-month experience of war reporting, chronicled in *Blind Date With Mars*, Alice-Leone went to Spain and from there sneaked into German-occupied Paris to further report on the war for *Collier's*, the *Herald Tribune*, and CBS. This adventure resulted in *No Passport for Paris*.

When asked what made her a successful writer, Alice-Leone replied emphatically, "I was extremely good-looking, and the men did anything for me that I wanted. Besides, I was intelligent." Alice-Leone did not classify herself as a journalist. "I *did not* study journalism. I don't think anyone should study journalism. You learn to write by writing, and by being coached, as editors used to do for their reporters." In addition, Alice-Leone said, "I was adventuresome. I've never been afraid of anything in my life."

Alice-Leone was born in 1908 in Mexico. "Both my parents were highly intelligent and adored me, an only child." Her father was a successful business man. Her mother had ambitious plans for Alice-Leone; she wanted her to speak five languages. By the time Alice-Leone went to an exclusive private school in New York at the age of twelve, she was indeed fluent in five languages. One year later she and her mother returned to Mexico, where she studied with tutors once again. Then mother and daughter traveled to Europe and Alice-Leone studied at the Convent of the Assumption both in Rome and Paris. "I wasn't a Catholic," she explained, "but that's where people thought they could get the best education."

Her education continued at the American School in Mexico and in a boarding school in South Carolina. Subsequently she lived in New York and continued to travel a great deal. Her first book appeared in 1933. *No Nice Girl Swears*, an etiquette book for girls, became a best seller.

Alice-Leone then began writing articles for magazines. In 1939 she did a profile on George Abbott, a renowned producer, and this launched another angle of her writing career. "I started doing a lot of interviews and profiles for magazines." It was these articles that gave her credibility as a journalist.

In 1940 Alice-Leone requested that *Collier's Weekly* send her to Russia. "A combination of the gambling spirit and ignorance made me a foreign correspondent," she wrote. The gambling spirit belonged to the editors of *Collier's Weekly*; the ignorance was mine."[1] She said that probably never had a reporter set out knowing less. She had not worked on a newspaper, she did not know how to file a piece, and her passport read, "Occupation, none." She listed her assets for this assignment as determination, a good memory, experience in traveling, fluency in five languages, and curiosity. She wrote in her book, *Blind Date With Mars*, "This is merely the story of a bit of small fry taking a trip round the world under the extraordinary conditions that prevailed in the Orient, Soviet Russia, and Africa during 1940 and 1941."[2]

"I got in as a tourist," Alice-Leone said, "and after a great deal of trouble had my status changed to correspondent."

The only way to get to Moscow, her intended destination, was to go via the Far East. Her first stop was Tokyo, and she described in detail her observations of prewar Japan—food, entertainment, clothing (including lack of silk to be purchased), education, religion, fellow travelers, and politics. She did this with a light touch and a satirical tone. At one point she wrote, "All these goings on [prewar exercises] didn't make sense to me, but then very little in Japan did."[3] She admitted that she didn't go to Japan with an open mind; although she hadn't known any "Japs," she disliked them by instinct. Her two-month stay proved her instincts correct, she believed.

All the time Alice-Leone was in Tokyo she attempted to get a visa from the Soviet Embassy. Her forced, extended stay was not dull, however, because she managed to meet many important people and go to interesting places. Finally, on very short notice, she received word from *Collier's* that she was to go to Hong Kong, take a look at the Burma Road, and proceed to Indo-China. She discovered that she couldn't fulfill the request from *Collier's* due to lack of transportation going to those locations in that order, so she settled for Indo-China and sailed from Tokyo in November of 1940.

First Alice-Leone stopped at Shanghai, where she enjoyed every moment of her stay. From there she sailed to Saigon, and reported on revolts against the French and events in surrounding Far Eastern countries, as well as Japanese involvement in those events. While in Rangoon, she received a cable from *Collier's*, stating, "As you don't seem to be getting to Russia return home immediately or send in final expense account."[4] Alice-Leone cabled back the vague answer, "Starting soonest," and proceeded on to Burma in January of 1941.[5]

Until February of 1941 Alice-Leone traveled across Burma, and finally embarked across China to Kunming. Then she went by plane to Chungking, the wartime capital of China. She spent several restless weeks until she finally received permission to leave for Moscow. She arrived at her long-anticipated destination in late May.

In Moscow Alice-Leone had an ongoing battle with the American ambassador and the censors. She described the censors as oriental language experts, but by no means experts at English. She said, "They spoke mostly cablese." One correspondent described the German army as being "downbogged," and when the censor couldn't find that word in the dictionary he asked what it meant. The correspondent replied that it was two words, "bogged down." So the censor looked up "bogged," and when he found "marsh" in the definition, he demanded that the word be changed in the news article. " 'There are no marshes near Smolensk,' he said."[6]

While in Moscow, Alice-Leone finagled privileges out of officials and talked with Soviet citizens, getting stories that she cabled back to the United States and later used in her book, *Blind Date With Mars*. As the war itself came nearer to Moscow she received numerous commands to return home. She described the German bombings and the heroism and courage of the Moscow citizens. On one occasion she and another correspondent watched the raids from an open window, something which at that point was forbidden. Searchlights lit up the sky, incendiary bombs fell, enemy planes came in groups of three, and Alice-Leone got so excited she leaned out of the window and yelled, "Get it! Shoot it down!" Her fellow correspondent caught her before she could topple out. Air raids, she said, always caused her to be sleepy, and she had to spend the night in this colleague's apartment. In the darkness he tried to help her fix up a bed on the sofa, saying that he didn't know if what they were using for bedding was sheets or tablecloths. Alice-Leone discovered in the morning that they had struck a pretty good average—one sheet and one tablecloth.

Conditions finally became such that Alice-Leone had to leave Moscow in October of 1941. She traveled by train to Kuibyshev and stayed there until November. Finally, she journeyed to Teheran, Baghdad, and various British colonies in Africa.

Alice-Leone returned to the United States in early 1942 and went on to Mexico to chronicle her adventures. At home, she enjoyed many things she had dreamed about during her trek around the world—such as plays, movies, dancing to good music, lying in hot, perfumed baths, shopping, eating huge beefsteaks, feasting her eyes on well-dressed people—and reveled in these luxuries for several months. "But suddenly, with the eccentricity typical of all foreign correspondents, I want only to go off on another assignment. The delays connected with getting away seem interminable. I can't wait to start off for places where none of those luxuries exist."[7]

In April of 1944 she did go on another assignment. She traveled to Spain and reported on conditions in that neutral country. Then she wanted to report on Paris under German occupation, so she hired guides to lead her there. She walked over the Pyrenees Mountains, led by members of the French Underground. This risky trek cost her $3,000. Once in Paris she blended in with the French, because "I spoke perfect French," she explained. After spending three weeks in Paris, she returned to Spain, then went on to Portugal and finally came back to the United States. She wrote her book, *No Passport for Paris*, and with that volume concluded her reporting of World War II.

However, she continued her career as a free-lance writer, producing a number of books and continuing to sell articles to magazines. She lived in New York for a while, frequently went abroad, and also lived in Mexico on occasion. In 1955 she moved to Washington. After spending two years there she left for Rome in 1957 and for the next eleven years lived and worked there. The *National Review* and *Newsday* paid for her articles and expenses. In 1969 she went on to Paris and wrote for the English section of *Le Monde*. Finally she returned to the United States in 1974. By then both her parents were deceased and she settled in Philadelphia. She currently writes a weekly column for the *Philadelphia Inquirer*.

In commenting on how she fared as a woman correspondent during her World War II experiences, she said, "There was a great advantage to being a female." When asked if she capitalized on her good looks, she declared, "You bet I did!"

NOTES

1. Alice-Leone Moats, *Blind Date With Mars* (Garden City, N.Y.: Doubleday Doran and Company, 1943), 3.
2. Ibid., 4.
3. Ibid., 32.
4. Ibid., 99.
5. Ibid.
6. Ibid., 266.
7. Ibid., 486.

11

Sigrid Schultz

"What to do with a woman on the board of the Foreign Press Club was quite a problem to official Germany." So wrote Sigrid Schultz in some brief autobiographical notes found in the *Chicago Tribune* archives. "Formerly one solved the woman's question by simply ignoring them or possibly inviting them to a vacuous tea. Staff affairs, 'beer evenings,' kept women out. But with a woman on the board of the club one simply had to modernize the official attitude and the women were invited to all functions. Even 'Bierabend.' "[1] This singular problem that Sigrid encountered in the 1920s was typical of many situations she faced and conquered as a woman journalist and as a war correspondent.

Sigrid was the daughter of a noted European portrait painter, Herman Schultz, who was of Norwegian origin. Her parents came to America for the 1893 World's Fair; her father was invited to paint the official portrait of the mayor of Chicago, Carter H. Harrison, Jr., for the fair. Sigrid was born in Chicago but moved back to Europe with her parents at the age of seven. Her father had studios in Paris (where the family lived), Cairo, London, and Berlin. She received her education in Paris and Berlin.

When World War I began, she and her mother were visiting her father's Berlin studio. As aliens, they had to report to the German police each day. She was an American citizen by birth, and her parents had acquired their citizenship papers during their stay in Chicago.

Sigrid's father was well known and respected, and his studio was generally a place where interesting people liked to come and talk politics. Sigrid acquired a good knowledge of the political situation in Germany at that time, and wrote brief commentaries of these situations in an autobiographical sketch. She told of the misery and hunger, especially of children and older men and women. Although rich

Sigrid Schultz. Copyrighted, Chicago Tribune Company, all rights reserved. Used with permission.

tourists would be willing to help the children, they had only scorn for the elderly who clutched their forlorn-looking dogs while trying to sell them because they could not feed them. She commented on "the old people and their last joy, the understanding mongrel bravely starving with them . . . a life of heartache for dog and master if they separated, slow death for both of them if they stayed together."2 Sigrid became keenly aware of both political and social issues, and these would become major topics in her subsequent writings.

Sigrid joined the *Chicago Tribune*'s Berlin bureau in 1919 as an interpreter—she was skilled in five languages. She also served as a secretary, a position she worked to leave behind as quickly as possible. By 1926 she was appointed bureau chief, probably the first woman to hold such a position in a major news bureau. In a book published in 1934, Ishbel Ross wrote, "She is popular with all her colleagues and is the only American newspaper woman running a news bureau in Europe today."3 In 1938 she took on duties with Mutual Broadcasting and did live broadcasts from Berlin.

One of these broadcasts was reported by the *Chicago Tribune* in August of 1939. "The Tribune's correspondent in Berlin gave a word picture of war preparations in the German capital and described the reactions of humbler citizens to Fuehrer Hitler's pact with Russia."4 Germans believed, Sigrid said, that Russia's full military and economic strength would be available to support Germany in case of a conflict. She described the anti-aircraft guns that were being put into place in Berlin for defense, saying that "the anti-aircraft boys in blue-grey uniforms tonight roar through Berlin in their trucks, reserving most of their glances and their broadest smiles for the girls who watch them pass."5

Sigrid was one of the first U.S. journalists to predict the coming major conflict—World War II.6 She had covered central Europe from 1916, and would do so until 1941. She interviewed many top Nazi leaders and "warned early of the dangers they represented to world peace and the lives of Jews in Hitler's Third Reich."7

She interviewed Hitler several times. During one interview he said to her, "You cannot understand the Nazi movement, because you think with your head and not with your heart."8 At another harrowing interview he shouted at her, "My will shall be done!"9 In July of 1939 she described Hitler's fascination with astrology. She wrote of Hitler's observatory six thousand feet above sea level in the Bavarian Alps. Astrology, she said, "is not a pastime. Hitler is known to regard it as a serious matter. For years he has enlisted the cooperation of German astrologers and outstanding men and women of kindred sciences."[10] The astrologers predicted, Sigrid reported, that Germany would be happy and all-powerful.

She wrote a book in 1944, *Germany Will Try It Again*, published by Reynal and Hitchcock, which spoke against the evils of Nazi Germany. In reviewing this book, William L. Shirer wrote, "No other American correspondent in Berlin knew so much of what was going on behind the scenes as did Sigrid Schultz."[11] Quentin Reynolds called her "Hitler's Greatest Enemy."

Her "very nasty stories" about the Germans caused threats to be made against her. "I told them to go ahead, . . . I said to them that if I were tossed out I would finally get a little rest and that I would make a wonderful martyr."[12] The Nazis allowed her to stay in Germany, but she never felt quite safe and would not drive a car because the Gestapo cars were outfitted with a specially built ramming device, and the Nazis could threaten or kill victims by ramming a car and pushing it over a bridge.

The Germans refused to let Sigrid go to the war front, both because she was a woman and because she had written anti-Nazi stories. "She was called the 'Dragon from Chicago' after she thwarted Goering's propaganda men in an attempt to plant spy documents in her apartment, part of a plan to harass correspondents and make an example of her."[13]

Sigrid's father had died in the 1920s, and she had sent her mother back to the United States in 1933, to a cottage in Westport, Connecticut. Sigrid herself returned to the United States in 1941 because of a shrapnel injury in her knee, a result of a radio broadcast during a Berlin bombing. In addition, she had picked up typhus and almost died from that illness.

In March of 1941 the *Chicago Tribune* printed an article by Sigrid in which she told of her experiences and impressions on her travels through Switzerland, France, Spain, and Portugal on her way to America. "The trip from war to peace," she wrote, "thru countries trembling in fear of what the next day will bring is arduous, but it provides a clear picture of what war means to the whole of continental Europe."[14]

After recuperating, she began a nationwide lecture tour, speaking against the evils of Nazi Germany. She was quite well known and well respected because of her very strong anti-German stand. An article in the *Chicago Tribune*, written in March 1941, reported one of Sigrid's lectures. Her comments were summarized: "If a Nazi surprise campaign now being planned is successful, Britain will be brought to her knees and the war will be over in three months. If this campaign does not come off, the world may expect a long war—at least three more years."[15] The article went on to describe the overflow crowd that listened to her share information that "had been communicated to her by her best-informed news sources in Berlin before she left the German capital several weeks ago."[16]

In 1944 she returned as a war correspondent for *McCall's* and *Liberty* magazines and was attached to the First and Third Armies. "She covered the Battle of the Ruhr with the First American Army and was with the first group of Americans to enter Berlin."[17] She also was one of the first liberators to arrive at Buchenwald. After the war she covered the Nuremberg war trials.

Over fifty years of age by the time the war ended, Sigrid returned to the United States and retired, both so she could take care of her mother and write. She was a very good judge of political situations and had an excellent sense of news stories, but she was not a good writer; after all, she had not had any training in journalism. The news she sent to her editors was excellent, but regrettably needed much editing, and eventually she could not get her material published because of this reason. In addition, Sigrid remained very anti-German after the war, and many magazines became unwilling to publish her material. She could never accept that people's attitudes had changed overnight, and that now the United States had become allies with Germany and had turned against the Russians. After the war, her notoriety and power diminished greatly, and she literally dropped out of sight. Even her colleagues in journalism avoided her because of her obsession with Germany. She would become quite irate if accused of being a German, which sometimes happened because of her name.

Sigrid was a no-nonsense woman and never let the fact that she was a female stand in the way of any advancement. Although scarcely five feet tall, and at times described as a "blonde beauty," she would never tolerate being treated any differently than a man would have been in a given situation.

She was a founder of the Overseas Press Club and active with that organization until she became an invalid. She remained in the little 250-year-old cottage she had found for her mother. This was a little house in the middle of town, which she liked because she didn't have to drive to do her shopping (her phobia about the Gestapo cars remained with her). The town wanted to buy her home and turn it into a parking lot, but she wouldn't allow it. "I was allowed to stay in this silly little house as long as I live, and then it goes to the town."18 At the time of her death in 1980 she was working on a history of German anti-Semitism.

EXCERPT FROM AN AUTOBIOGRAPHICAL SKETCH BY SIGRID SCHULTZ (COPIED EXACTLY FROM HER ORIGINAL)

The death of a present [sic; president] new elections stand out in the news line. When President Ebert died, the story came quite smoothly. Thanks to journalistic luck I was terribly sick when the report spread that Ebert had been operated on. Nobody could get into the hospital. Shivering with fever, without a voice, I had crawled down to the office being convinced that the best cure for bronchitis is work. Then John Clayton told me that all the other fellows were trying to get to the hospital but that everybody was barred. I took up the receiver of the telephone, and with my raucous sick voice told the reception nurse of the hospital that my doctor had ordered me to their home and that I would come in an hour, to please have everything in order. I looked up the list of doctors of the hospital. One name sounded familiar, but the thing was to get on the same floor as Ebert. Therefore when I arrived at the hospital I pretended to have forgotten the doctors name. I was locked up in a waiting room without any chance of prowling around as I had hoped to. After a useless quarter of an hour, I remembered the doctor's name and went to the nurse. "Which one, the young one or the old one?" said the nurse. I lost my voice to gain time. "Don't you know how your doctor looks?" said she suspiciously, but I looked so dumb and so weak that her suspicions dwindled. I finally decided for the younger doctor. Locked myself up in my room to be sure not to be thrown out. When the doctor came, he told me that my heart was in a most terrible condition, I must remain stretched out without moving for at least ten days. Then I exploded and told the man what I had come for. He was a good sport. We made an agreement. I was to remain stretched out with the permission to nose around a little—but very little—and to swallow everything served to me and the doctor would act as reporter. He was no good reporter—but a good doctor. He had a long conference with the assistants who had been present at the Ebert operation and told me two days before Ebert's death that he had no chance whatever. The Official bulletins were all about Ebert's recovery. My great fear was that Ebert might die toward morning, when there was still a chance of getting one word over in time for the final edition. So I spent my nights prowling around the nurse's kitchen until the nuns were convinced that there was something wrong in my mind. Lemonade was Ebert's last drink at two o'clock in the morning. I know, because I was in the kitchen telling the night nurse that the nurses on my floor had disappeared and would she please give me lemonade. "I'm making some for Ebert," said she, "and you can have some of it." And quite excited she added "I was a monarchist until today but now I am a republican. The President is the gentlest patient I ever had" and off she marched with the President's last lemonade. Quietly telephoning out my reports, I watched the assistants of the other American offices in Berling trying to crash the gate of the Santorium, marching up and down before the door by the hour hoping for somebody who knew to come out and give them the scoop.

NOTES

1. Sigrid Schultz, autobiographical notes from the *Tribune* archives.
2. Ibid.
3. Ishbel Ross, *Ladies of the Press* (New York: Harper, 1936; reprint 1974), 377.
4. "Tribune Writer Says Red Pact Tickles Berlin," *Chicago Tribune*, 25 August 1939.
5. Ibid.
6. "Sigrid Schultz, 87, Hitler's Enemy," *Overseas Press Club Bulletin*, 1 June 1980, p. 1.
7. "Sigrid Schultz Is Dead; Early Berlin Correspondent," *Chicago Tribune*, 16 May 1980.
8. Ibid.
9. M.L. Stein, *Under Fire: The Story of American War Correspondents* (New York: Julian Messner, 1968), 215.
10. Sigrid Schultz, "Hitler Gazes at Stars to Guide His Decisions," *Chicago Tribune*, 13 July 1939.
11. "Sigrid Schultz . . . Hitler's Enemy."
12. Stein, *Under Fire*.
13. Marion Marzolf, *Up from the Footnote* (New York: Hastings House, 1977), 70.
14. Sigrid Schultz. "Crossing Europe to Peace! A View by Miss Schultz," *Chicago Tribune*, 1 March 1941.
15. "Sigrid Schultz Sees Blitz—Or A 3 Year War," *Chicago Tribune*, 5 March 1941.
16. Ibid.
17. Stein, *Under Fire*, 216.
18. Joseph Egelhof, "A Celebrated Voice of Experience Speaks Out Against Nazi Dangers," *Chicago Tribune*, 28 November 1977.

12

Inez Robb

Inez Robb and Ruth Cowan were the first American women to be accredited as war correspondents at the time of the North African invasion in 1943. This accomplishment probably was not seen as unusual by Inez herself. In later years she was to give counsel in her newspaper column to young people who wanted careers in journalism. They should, she wrote, develop hides as tough as that of a rhinoceros. Inez was known for her tough hide, even though she had been described as pretty, with Irish blue eyes (something she admitted was not a handicap), and she had a witty style.

Inez Callaway was born on a 15,000-acre cattle ranch in Middletown, California. Her grandfathers were southerners and forty-niners, and her father was in a fruit-packing business. Later, these humble beginnings would amuse her as she achieved fame writing the society pages. She grew up in Caldwell, Idaho, a town of four thousand people not far from Boise and got her first newspaper job when she was fifteen as a high school correspondent for the *Capital News* in Boise. This allowed her to buy the silk stockings she wanted—something her parents thought was frivolous.

She attended the University of Idaho on a scholarship and earned money by writing social news—an easy task because her aunt was a socialite in the area. Next, she studied journalism at the University of Missouri and graduated from that school in 1924. She then became a general assignment reporter with the Tulsa, Oklahoma, *Daily World* with a salary of $40 a week; she stayed with this job for twenty-seven months.

Then Inez left for Chicago, her scrapbook under her arm. Captain Joseph M. Patterson, the publisher, hired her, then offered her a higher salary, almost double what she got in Oklahoma, to work on the Sunday edition of the *New York Daily News*. She worked for eighteen months as assistant editor. In May 1928, the *News* society editor left, and she was asked to take the job. The idea didn't suit her. " 'How in the world could I be a society reporter?' Miss Callaway protested. 'I don't even like champagne and I buy my hats in bargain basements.' 'Well, try it for three weeks to tide us over,' said an unsympathetic editor.' "[1] If she really disliked the work as much as she thought she would, she could return to the general news desk.

Inez wrote under the byline of Nancy Randolph, which was the *Tribune*'s syndicated name for the society column. Writing in a joking tone that no one objected to, she was "fearless, witty and bright. . . . Her column has a gay, amusing tang. And her eyes are as perceptive as they are blue."[2]

She set a pattern that would be adopted by other society columnists. "I just did a good reporting job," she explained later. "I never ridiculed anybody; I don't think any newspaper writer has a right to do that."[3]

Inez "brought to this usually quiet spot a vitality and an excitement by treating society affairs as real news."[4] She didn't write just from her desk, as did some society reporters of her time. She decided quickly that she had to put faces behind the names that cropped up in the society pages, and she worked like a police reporter, writing from the scene. When she failed to be invited to the wedding of Percy Rockefeller's daughter, she circumvented that problem. About an hour and a half before the service started, a woman with a mourning veil came into the church and knelt in fervent prayer. Ushers didn't have the heart to banish her, so when the wedding took place, Inez got a clear picture, in spite of her mourning veil, of what took place and the next morning's newspaper readers got the same.

Her attitude with subjects for her society column was "I have no power to keep your name out of my paper. . . . As long as you make news, I shall use it."[5] She covered stories such as the coronation of King George VI in London, the wedding of the Duke and Duchess of Windsor, and the opening of the Paris Exposition in 1937.[6]

In 1929 Inez Callaway married Major J. Addison Robb, and she continued writing her column for the *Daily News*. As a report about her in *Editor and Publisher* said, "But her marriage did not keep her from her chosen calling."[7] In 1938 she joined International News Service and began writing a column, "Assignment: America," which appeared daily in the Hearst newspapers throughout America.

Her stories included much travel. In 1939 Pan American Airlines began European service, and Inez flew on its first round-trip flight across the Atlantic.

Then World War II began. Inez was eventually able to join the ranks of war correspondents and she boarded a ship in January of 1943, along with the first two companies of the Women's Auxiliary Army Corps being sent to the war zone. She and Ruth Cowan, who had also been sent to North Africa, received an icy reception in Algiers from Wes Gallagher, chief of the Associated Press bureau. He, along with many others, did not approve of women war correspondents.

Inez was allowed to visit the front, going by plane to Tunisia. She and Ruth Cowan watched the American forces retreat with the advance of the German armies under the command of General Rommel.[8] Because of the confusion, their plane left without them and they had to catch a ride back to Algiers on a truck. In spite of these kinds of mishaps, the women correspondents managed to send outstanding stories back to their wire services, and as a result received accolades for their achievements. They had the distinctive honor of being compared to Ernie Pyle because of their ability to be descriptive in conveying the details and mood of an event.

Inez returned to New York, her job, and her husband before the war was over. After the war, Inez set a record—something she would later describe as "one of the silliest in the books." When world tourist service was resumed, she was one of three reporters to fly around the world in six days—proving that the human body can outlast an airplane, she said later.

She returned to Germany in 1946, then journeyed to Argentina and Chile, where she interviewed Peron and two Chilean presidents. The first resigned on the same day she interviewed him.

Back in the United States in the fall of 1946, Inez flew to Texas City to write about the series of explosions that leveled the harbor. She went to the waterfront, and was just in time to be knocked off her feet by another explosion, one that flattened the taxi she had just left. She wrote her story and alarmed the INS editors, who warned her to be more cautious. She wired back, "No more 'Perils of Pauline' for me . . . I'm getting too old to be blown out of my nylons at three o'clock in the morning."[9]

In England she reported on the marriage of Princess Elizabeth in 1947; she was one of few journalists allowed to cover the event as an eyewitness. She received the George R. Holmes Memorial Award for distinguished reporting for this story; she was the first woman to receive this award.[10] In 1953 she returned to cover the coronation of Queen Elizabeth II.

Also in 1953 Inez left INS and began to write a column for Scripps-Howard and United Feature Syndicate. *Editor and Publisher* reported, "The major talent switch, one of the biggest in recent years and reversing the traditional acquisition of stars by Hearst, was negotiated by Jack R. Howard, president of the Scripps-Howard Newspapers."[11] She covered a wide range of topics such as the Hungarian freedom fighters, TV "pitchmen," American fashion at that time enslaved to Paris, and the Brussels World's Fair. She continued to write from both stateside and foreign lands.

Inez received many honors for her columns, including the New York Newspaper Women's Club award for the "best column in any field." She continued to be active in the field of journalism until her death in 1980. Once she said, " 'I love my work. I guess I was just born to be a newspaperwoman and I'd hate to be out of the mainstream of the news."[12]

NOTES

1. Ishbel Ross, *Ladies of the Press* (New York: Harper, 1936; reprint 1974), 451.
2. Ibid., 450.
3. Quoted in *Current Biography 1958.*
4. "Inez Robb's Column," *Editor and Publisher*, 24 October 1953, p. 8.
5. Ross, *Ladies*, 451.
6. "Inez Robb's Column."
7. Ibid.
8. M.L. Stein, *Under Fire: The Story of American War Correspondents* (New York: Julian Messner, 1968), 218; and Edwin Emery and Michael Emery, *The Press and America: An Interpretative History of the Mass Media (Englewood Cliffs, N.J.: Prentice-Hall, 1978), 340.*
9. "Inez Robb's Column."
10. "Inez Robb Wins Award," *New York Times*, 5 February 1948.
11. "Inez Robb's Column."
12. Ibid.

13

Sonia Tomara

"I never demanded anything for being a woman or expected to have any preference over men. I was doing my work as any man would have done. I didn't see why I should ask for more." These were Sonia Tomara's sentiments about her experiences as a war correspondent, and these statements also reflected her productive life as a journalist. As far as being a war correspondent, she added, "During the war, it was easy because many men had been called to the colors. Women had an advantage in journalism then."[1]

Sonia Tomara was born in 1897 in St. Petersburg, Russia. Her parents were White Russians who owned large estates in the Caucasian Mountains before the revolution. Her father was highly educated and tutored Sonia at home until she enrolled in the University of Moscow. As was typical of that time, especially for children from high-class families, Sonia learned several languages. This capability was to be a distinct advantage when she became a journalist and subsequently a war correspondent.

The Russian Revolution caused many like Sonia's family to flee and she, her mother, and two sisters escaped on freight trains from St. Petersburg to the south. Her father stayed behind and was never heard from again. The women sailed on a U.S. destroyer leaving from Batoum and arrived in Constantinople. Because Sonia could speak Turkish she found work with the British High Commission. One year later the women went to Paris. With only 150 francs left, Sonia realized she had to go to work in order to provide for an elderly mother and her sisters, who were not as well equipped as she to be employed. She soon found work with *Le Matin*, a French newspaper.

She began as secretary to the foreign editor and quickly became assistant to him. Before long she was in charge because of his frequent absences and "soon plunged into international political reporting as well as financial affairs which led to writing a weekly financial review for the *Herald Tribune* and to an assignment in its Paris bureau."[2] After joining the *Herald Tribune* staff in 1928 on a permanent basis, she accompanied the Rome correspondent, John T. Whitaker, to Italy. Sent there by her boss, Leland Stowe, then head of the Paris bureau, "she landed at a moment when news was breaking fast, and soon her stories were leading the paper, some days with three-column heads, a rare distinction for a woman in the foreign field."[3]

Before long Sonia became a regular on the *Herald Tribune* staff. When President Doumer was assassinated only three blocks from her office, she was one of the first reporters on the scene. She went to the hospital where the president was taken, and soon had the details she needed for a front-page story. She was in Munich during the Hitler revolt and again demonstrated how she could collect facts with accuracy and rapidity. At that time, as well as many others, she gave evidence of being a shrewd political commentator. The fact that she was a hard worker was well known, and she was particularly respected because she could switch from French to Spanish to German to Italian to English without difficulty, and thereby get the story quicker and better than most of her peers.

In 1937 Sonia was invited to join the *Tribune* staff in New York, but in 1939 she returned to Europe and became a roving correspondent, traveling throughout southeastern Europe.

With Marylla Chrzanowska of Associated Press, she "reported from Warsaw during the German blitzkrieg, narrowly missing death."[4] " 'I was deadly scared,' she admitted. 'It's not glamorous to write eyewitness stories about the collapse of an heroic Polish capital or about the heart-rending sufferings of the Polish refugees.' "[5] Sonia also reported on the fighting in the Balkans.

Sonia went to Paris in May of 1940 to cover the German invasion of France. By June she and her sister Irina had to flee the city because of the imminent approach of the German armies. Their car broke down and they caught rides on trucks that were part of the exodus. A few days later the Germans conquered Paris. Sonia, who had her typewriter with her, hiked back to a town where she could cable a story to the *Tribune*. She wrote her story, found a censor, and then returned to search for her sister, whom she had left sitting on a pile of luggage amidst the flow of fleeing humanity. They continued their flight, while Sonia's story became front-page news in the *Herald Tribune*.

Having fled to Portugal, Sonia requested an American assignment and came to New York in 1938. Kathleen McLaughlin was among the first to befriend Sonia. After all the major stories she had covered in Europe, her first major assignment was to write about a cat show! She later said it was humiliating, but it taught her something about reporting in America and the big city.

In 1942 Sonia received accreditation as a war correspondent and went to the China-Burma-India theater. She covered the political and military situation in this area. When a British governor of Ceylon asked how she, a woman, got there, she replied, "I was like the British. I didn't know when I was licked!"[6] As the only woman correspondent in India, she had a fascinating time even though not a great deal was happening. She traveled throughout India and flew to China over the Himalayan Mountains. She was in Calcutta when the Japanese bombed that city in December of 1942. In May of 1943 she traveled to China on the Yangtze River and stayed in that area for three months. On most of these ventures she was the only woman correspondent, which caused problems and yet had advantages. "Being the only woman in a 'man's world,' you attract attention," she stated later.[7]

Sonia's greatest desire was to fly on a bombing mission and she requested permission to do so from General Stilwell, the commanding general of this war theater. At first he wouldn't hear of it, then said maybe. Thinking she had clearance from him, she approached General Chennault who said, "Why not?" since she was an accredited war correspondent. An exciting mission resulted in a story and aroused the anger of a public relations officer in Chungking, who reported her to Stilwell. Fearing his wrath and that she would be disaccredited, she wrote a letter of apology, saying she thought permission had been granted by proper authorities. He wrote back and said, "We like you and it's all right."[8]

In 1943 she cabled greetings to the New York Newspaper Women's Club and said, "It was not easy to get accreditation, but since I was passed the American Army gave me the same facilities as men. I have traveled some 30,000 miles in Army planes, and I have been in air fields, barracks and Army messes. . . . There is an air-raid warning as I write this, and I can see people from the town fleeing for miles."[9] At that time she also expressed the hope that there would be more women war correspondents in foreign posts: "I am confident they will do as well as men, if not better."[10]

Sonia also expressed her feelings about being a war correspondent: "Never have I ceased to enjoy for a minute this assignment, one of the grandest of my life."[11]

From the China-Burma-India theater of war Sonia went on to Cairo in late 1943 and wrote about meetings of the major powers. She then proceeded to Teheran and Algiers, spending six months in the latter place. In the summer of 1944 she returned to Paris and was reunited with her family. It was a glorious time, since she had fled Paris under war conditions and could now return to a liberated city. The following year she returned to New York, resigned from the *Herald Tribune*, and married Federal Judge William Clark, whom she had met in Algiers.

In commenting on her experiences as a war correspondent, Sonia said,

> I never tried to have scoops, because a scoop lives one day and dies the next. Newspaper articles last only one day. You don't have to have any illusions about that. I think it's more important to cover the events behind the scene rather than the obvious, which everybody covers. Any foreign correspondent for a serious paper wants to cover history, or at least have the illusion that he or she covers history.[12]

Sonia died in 1982.

A SAMPLE OF WAR REPORTING BY SONIA TOMARA

ON THE ROADS OF FRANCE

TOURS, France, June 14.—For four days and four nights I have shared the appalling hardship of 5,000,000 French refugees who are now fleeing down all the roads of France leading to the south. My story is the typical story of nine-tenths of these refugees.

I left Paris Monday night, June 10, in a big car which was to take me, my sister, Irene Tomara, and a Canadian doctor, William Douglas, who has been working with the American and civilian refugees. We loaded our car with whatever we could carry. We had enough gasoline to take us at least to Bordeaux. It was quite dark when we left. All days cars had been going toward the southern gates of Paris. Just as we departed dark clouds rose above the town, obscuring the rising crescent of the moon. I thought at first it was a storm. Then I understood it was a smoke screen the French had laid down to save the city from bombing.

We drove across the Seine bridge and in complete darkness past the Montparnasse station, in which a desperate crowd was camping. We found the so-called Italian Gate and drove past it, risking all the time the chance of being hit by trucks. But all went well for about fifteen miles. Then, as we started up the first hill, the gears of our car refused to work and the car would not move.

We managed to pull off the road and park. We were in a small suburb of Paris. As nothing could be done during the dark hours, we rolled into our sleeping bags in a ditch alongside the road and tried to sleep. But cars roared by us incessantly. Then came an air-raid alarm. Then the cars started again.

When dawn came we tried to get the car going. It would not start. We waited for hours for a mechanic, while cars passed at the rate of twenty a minute. Then we learned there were no mechanics. They had all been called into the army. But the driver of a truck stopped and inspected the car. He said it could not be repaired on the road.

We tried to buy a little truck that could take our luggage. Finally the gendarmes on the road took pity on us and stopped a military truck, asking its driver to tow us. Fortunately we had a chain. We started off at noon on the road to Fontainebleau. At that time the road was a dense stream of army and factory trucks carrying big machines. We drove all day, and at 8 P.M. got into Fontainebleau.

In Fontainebleau we located a garage. The mechanic looked at the car and said it could not be repaired in less than two days. "We have no men to repair it, anyway," the manager of the garage said. "We work only for the army." We passed the night at a hotel and in the morning started to look for a truck that could tow us. Douglas found a youngster who had a country truck, but no gasoline. He was going back to Paris. We promised him gasoline and he said he would take us to Orleans and then drive to Paris.

We were abandoning our car, which was worth at least 40,000 francs (approximately $875), but money had ceased to have significance. We reloaded our bags on the truck, which had no top, and sat on them. It was 5 P.M. We drove five miles without difficulty and then got into a stream of refugees and army cars. Refugees blocked the road by trying to get past the main line of cars, thus interfering with oncoming traffic. At 10 P.M. we had driven less than fifteen miles from Fontainebleau. The boy driving our car was in despair. He wanted to turn back to Paris, but we would not let him. We saw thousands of cars by the roadsides, without gasoline or broken down.

We drove on in the night. Presently the road cleared, but we were off our route. Soldiers had detoured traffic to permit movement of military cars. We were driving south instead of toward Orleans. In a small village we turned off and started at a good speed through the dead of night, with lights turned off. It was fantastic. The clouds parted and the moon came up. The country seemed phantom-like. There were piles of stones in front of each village we passed, and peasants with rifles guarded these barricades. They looked at our papers and let us pass.

We arrived before the Orleans station at 3 A.M. on Thursday. After three nights and two days we had made only seventy miles. The scene near the station was appalling. People lay on the floor inside and the town square was filled. We piled our baggage and waited until daylight. There was nothing to eat in the town, no rooms in the hotels, no cars for sale or hire, no gasoline anywhere. Yet a steady stream of refugees was coming in, men, women and children, all desperate, not knowing where to go or how.

I walked around and found a truck that was fairly empty. I talked to the driver, offering him money to take me to Tours. He would take us near Tours. For food, we had only a little wine, some stale bread and a can of ham.

The scene of the refugees around the station was the most horrible I had ever seen, worse than the refugees in Poland. Fortunately, there was no bombing. Had there been any attacks it would have been too ghastly for words. Children were crying. There was no milk, no bread. Yet social workers were doing their best and groups were led away all the time, but new ones continued to arrive.

All morning we sought means of transportation. There was none. I decided to go to Tours. I started to walk in the rain with my typewriter and sleeping bag, at last getting a lift in a car which moved slowly through a mob of refugees moving in the opposite direction. In Tours, I learned that the government had left. Also gone were most newspapermen, but a press wireless operator and the French censor were still there.

As I finish this story there is a German air raid. The sound of bombs is terrific. I hope the German bombers have not hit at the road which leads to the south, for there refugees are packed in fleeing crowds. [Here eight words were censored.]

The catastrophe that has befallen France has no parallel in human history. Nobody knows how or when it will end. Like the other refugees, and there are millions of us, I do not know tonight when I shall sleep in a bed again, or how I shall get out of this town.

NOTES

1. Jean E. Collins, *She Was There: Stories of Pioneering Women Journalists* (New York: Julian Messner, 1980), 83–84.

2. Marion Marzolf, *Up from the Footnote* (New York: Hastings House, 1977), 70.

3. Ishbel Ross, *Ladies of the Press* (New York: Harper, 1936; reprint 1974), 372.

4. M.L. Stein, *Under Fire: The Story of American War Correspondents* (New York: Julian Messner, 1968), 237.

5. Marzolf, *Footnote*.

6. Collins, *She Was There*, 80.

7. Ibid., 82.

8. Ibid., 83.

9. "Awards Given by Newspaper Women's Club," *Herald Tribune*, 15 May 1943.

10. Ibid.

11. "Newspaper Club Cites Reporters," *New York Times*, 15 May 1943.

12. Collins, *She Was There*, 84.

14

Martha Gellhorn

"In the Second World War, all I did was praise the good, brave and generous people I saw, knowing this to be a perfectly useless performance." Martha Gellhorn wrote this in the 1959 introduction to her book, *The Face of War.*[1] "I took an absurd professional pride in getting where I intended to go and in sending my copy to New York on time; but I could not fool myself that my war correspondent's work mattered a hoot."[2] Yet she was to write about war a great deal. The contents of *The Face of War* as well as the material compiled in *The View From the Ground*, indicate her fascination, her involvement, her near-obsession with war.

She began her war correspondence with the war in Spain, continued through the war in Finland, the war in China, the Second World War, the war in Java, the war in Vietnam, the Six-Day War, and finally wars in Central America. "War is a malignant disease, an idiocy, a prison, and the pain it causes is beyond telling or imagining; but war was our condition and our history, the place we had to live in."[3] She further commented on her role during the many wars she covered: "I was a special type of profiteer; I was physically lucky, and was paid to spend my time with magnificent people."[4] Martha did indeed mingle with the excitement and drama of World War II, and with the people who were memorable at that time.

Martha Gellhorn was born on November 8, 1908, in St. Louis, Missouri. Her parents were distinguished and remarkable and provided a "loving, merry, stimulating" home, as Martha put it. Her father was a prominent gynecologist in St. Louis and was professor at both Washington and St. Louis universities. Her mother, a Bryn Mawr College graduate, spoke out for suffrage, with her husband's approval, and became very much involved in community and social causes.

Martha herself attended Bryn Mawr but dropped out at the end of her junior year. She held two jobs in the summer and fall of 1929, on the *New Republic* and the Hearst *Times Union* in Albany. Then she wrote an article for the *Holland America* trade paper which paid for her way to France. In this way she was working toward her lifelong goal—to become a foreign correspondent. She wrote that her "plan for life was to go everywhere, see everything, and write about it."[5]

First she worked for an advertising agency, then became a writer with *Vogue*, and finally joined the United Press bureau in Paris. At the same time she wrote her first novel. She had a dual purpose—fiction was her true ambition, while journalism would be a way to learn about and see the world.

She returned to America in the fall of 1934, concerned about the problems in her own country. She became a relief investigator for the Federal Emergency Relief Administration and visited the depressed mill towns of New England and the South. Through this work she became acquainted with the Roosevelts; she and Eleanor Roosevelt remained lifelong friends. The result of her work was *The Trouble I've Seen,* a book that achieved distinction as a literary work, and one that brought attention she did not want. She fled to Key West, where she met Ernest Hemingway (she would later become his third wife), and then to St. Louis, where she tried to write another novel. Frustrated with these efforts, she sailed for France again.

Martha joined Hemingway in Spain in March of 1937. She had received a letter from an editor at *Collier's* that she was a special correspondent for that magazine in Spain. She didn't place much significance in this letter as she became, she said, "a tourist of the war," traveling with a knapsack, the clothes on her back, and fifty dollars. She didn't file any stories but tagged along with the experienced war correspondents. Finally, a journalist friend asked why she didn't write a story—after all, she was a writer, wasn't she? She mailed her first article to *Collier's* and her name appeared on the masthead of that magazine. "Once on the masthead, I was evidently a war correspondent. It began like that."[6]

Once again Martha returned to the United States to work on behalf of the civil war going on in Spain. At that time she was a young visionary, believing she and her friends could indeed make a difference. She was described as generous, full of life, full of fun. Her slender figure and long shapely legs, as well as her tawny gold hair, attracted attention, but what often attracted more attention was her intensity of purpose when she found a cause and her determination to accomplish her self-appointed tasks well. She was demanding of herself.

In the late summer of 1937 she returned to Spain and wrote from the front. From here she first displayed her inclination to write about the tragedy of war, almost to the exclusion of other viewpoints. She was one of the correspondents requested by foreign networks to send out broadcasts. Some of these were heard by her mother in St. Louis. Then she reluctantly agreed to take on a lecture tour in the United States to raise money for Spanish medical aid. She traveled throughout the United States in early 1938, but after two months, frustrated by the futility of convincing comfortable American audiences to participate in "the cause," she fled back to Europe.

After Spain, she received assignments for *Collier's* in Czechoslovakia, England, and France, although her interest in the Spanish war still remained alive. The summer of 1938 was spent in Czechoslovakia and she produced a carefully documented report for *Collier's*. She fulfilled her assignments in England just as thoroughly and noted how England had always had the privilege of fighting her wars elsewhere, but now had to fight on her own territory. She drove to the Spanish and Italian frontiers and wrote that nowhere did she find any appetite for war—there were enough graves to last a lifetime. She returned to Spain and then traveled to Prague to determine for herself what was happening with the Czech people as their rulers capitulated to Hitler. Finally, she returned to the United States.

In October of 1939, with World War II now officially started, Martha received an inquiry from *Collier's* editor Charles Colebaugh about going to Finland. He felt something was about to happen there, with the Soviet Union making threatening moves along the border. Martha hesitated, but sailed in November on a small Dutch vessel. Most of the other passengers were anxious Europeans wondering what would happen in their own countries but a worry they all shared was the new magnetic mine. She landed in Belgium and flew to Helsinki on November 29, arriving there just hours ahead of the first bombing. She wrote that the Finns would fight a defensive war and not lose the country like the Czechs had. "I did think, professionally, that it was unusual timing to arrive in a strange frozen country one dark afternoon and be waked the next morning at nine o'clock by the first bombs, the declaration of war. But before the bombs, there were the sea and the mines. Looking back, nearly twenty years, it seems to me that my thinking or feeling about war changed again on that curious ocean journey."[7]

When Christmas Eve came, she had completed her *Collier's* assignment and had written articles about Sweden as well. By this time she was not only a seasoned war correspondent but an acclaimed novelist as well.

When her most recent book, *The Trouble I've Seen*, was publicized after her return to the United States, many aspects of her personality showed in the publicity shots—the slick, glamorous, fashionable person; the serious, austere, contemplative artist; and the active, happy person riding horses or playing tennis and wearing no makeup. But back at home her work wasn't going well. The grim news from Europe bothered her, and she traced the disasters on wall maps. *Collier's* urged her to return to the war scene.

Worried as she was about Europe, she wanted to see the Orient next. She had an immense curiosity, a quality that made her a fine journalist, and she wanted to see the Far East before she died, or the world came to an end, or whatever happened. "The Orient was across the world from what I loved and feared for. Journalism now turned into an escape route."8 She was assigned to report from Hong Kong, Singapore, the Dutch East Indies, and the Burma Road, and find out how the Sino-Japanese War progressed. No one knew, or cared much, about the war in China, she felt, and this made her curious.

By this time Martha had married Hemingway and he joined her during part of her Asian experience. Also by this time she had developed a reluctance to have her name connected with his, partly because of accusations that her growing fame was thanks to his.

She returned to the United States in June of 1941. Then came Pearl Harbor. Martha was with Hemingway in Arizona when they heard the news. She continued to work on a novel as well as write for *Collier's*, and her travels took her to the Caribbean and South America. In the fall of 1943 *Collier's* notified her that they would be sending her to London as an official war correspondent. She left on October 29 and arrived in London on November 3.

Martha's first stories came from England. From here she reported on British fliers, ordinary children who did the work normally done by men now in the war effort, and on the conditions of Jews in the Warsaw ghetto, as told to her by Polish refugees. Then she traveled to the Italian front, and over the mountainous area where villages had been leveled, yet where the survivors went on with life as usual.

During this time she requested that Hemingway join her and when he finally did, she learned what a formidable adversary he could be. Miffed that she had left him for months while she worked as a war correspondent, he offered his services to *Collier's*, where she had been employed since 1937. Because the rules of the U.S. press corps allowed for only one front-line correspondent per magazine, this move left Martha without a chance of covering the war in an official capacity. Hemingway flew to Europe, while Martha had to go over on a slow boat. When she met him in England, she severed their relationship.

Martha wrote, "From November 1943, with one unavoidable break in the spring of 1944, I followed the war wherever I could reach it."[9] She learned of the Allied invasion during a morning briefing in London. Ernest was with other accredited correspondents, while she had to fend for herself. Secretly she boarded an unarmed hospital ship that would cross the Channel at dawn, and under cover of darkness on the night of June 7, she went ashore with the others who collected the wounded men. She actually walked on the Normandy beachhead, while Ernest was confined to the bridge of a landing craft.[10] Naturally this infuriated Ernest. On July 22, 1944, his eyewitness account of the Normandy landing was *Collier's* front-page story, and Martha's description of the first hospital ship to reach Normandy after the invasion was modestly featured.

As expected, Martha was chastised for her illegal trip with the hospital ship to Normandy and ordered to an American nurses training camp in England. She could cross to France with the nurses, she was told. She tolerated this for a day, then climbed a fence and hitchhiked to the nearest military airfield. On the pretext of wanting to see her fiancé in Italy, she got a lift to Naples. "I had no papers, no travel orders, no PX rights, nothing. I was a gypsy in that war in order to report it," she said.[11] She wrote about this in *The Face of War*: "The U.S. Army public relations officers, the bosses of the American press, were a doctrinaire bunch who objected to a woman being a correspondent with combat troops. I felt like a veteran of the Crimean War by then, and I had been sent to Europe to do my job, which was not to report the rear areas or the woman's angle."[12]

She reported the war bravely and well. She went with units of the British Eighth Army, joined the Poles in the Adriatic, and shared hardships with French soldiers in Central Italy. She said, "By stealth and chicanery I managed to sneak to Holland and watch the superb U.S. 82nd Airborne Division at work. But it was only during the Battle of the Bulge, and from then on, that I dared attach myself to American fighting units. The war may have softened the P.R.O.s, or they no longer cared what anyone did, with the end so near."[13]

It was during the Battle of the Bulge that she flew with a night fighter, in freezing weather, searching for German war planes. The pilot found himself being shot at instead of doing the shooting. By some miracle he landed the plane safely, despite the air battle and terrible weather, and as a result Martha reported one more dramatic event she herself witnessed and experienced.

Before the war ended, the editor of *Collier's* died. Because she didn't like his successor, she resigned and decided she would free-lance from then on. Fiction still played an important part in her writing career, but she realized she would have to write news articles and features in order to make a living.

After the war ended, Martha "wondered what I would do with the rest of my life."14 By now she had already divorced Hemingway. She continued to travel throughout Europe and to write, reporting poignantly on the aftermath of the war. "In terms of life, the price falls most heavily where it is least deserved and least noticed—on children."15

She wanted to settle in London, where she felt most at peace, but then she received a letter from her mother, letting her know in no uncertain terms that if she did not return home before long, she would be an expatriate. Martha arrived in America in the spring of 1947. At first she enjoyed the comfort and convenience of being in America, but increasingly she became disturbed at aspects of the American system and American attitudes. She wrote of her frustration about American indifference to the war and its results:

> I do not see how anyone can make that reality [hunger, desolation, burned out buildings, hopelessly repaired clothes, and the like] clear to Americans, because they have not felt it and experience is not communicated through the mind. But if Americans could understand and feel that reality, someone should tell them to be generous quickly, to be impractically and imprudently generous, since it is not safe for one nation alone to be so blessed.16

In another article she wrote, "The war cannot be forgotten. It was a terrible war, inching over the land from Sicily to the Alps."17

Disillusioned and uncomfortable, she decided to leave America. "I was a foreign correspondent; logically foreign correspondents lived in foreign countries. The world was wide and much of it very lovely; I intended to suit myself from now on and if that made me an expatriate, see if I cared."18

She returned to London, where she felt she belonged, then went to write about the war in Java—by now wondering if she could write about anything else besides war. Following that she reported on the Vietnamese war, and with the sad conclusion that perhaps for the first time she reported from the wrong side—she was so disillusioned about America's attitudes and actions in that war. Subsequently she rushed to report on the Six-Day War in the Middle East, and finally she covered the wars in Central America.

In her book, *The Face of War*, she included three introductions, the last one dated 1986. In these introductions she pondered about journalism and the reporting of war. She wrote in 1959, "War is a horrible repetition."[19] She said she reported about ordinary people, and each of her selections in the book simply included examples of what happened to many, until all the stories she wrote blended into one appalling picture. "There is a single plot in war; action is based on hunger, homelessness, fear, pain and death."[20]

She wrote in her 1986 introduction about the paranoia of superpowers facing each other, and the effect this has on the human race. "An intolerable way to run the world. Intolerable for every one of us, all the people who live here."[21] In *The View From the Ground*, she closed her commentary on the forties by saying, "If people who ran the world could not run it without wars and if the people who lived in the world did not rebel against such deadly incompetence, I personally declared a separate peace."[22]

Martha achieved respect both as a foreign correspondent and as a novelist. She continues to reside outside of the United States and currently lives in Wales.

A SAMPLE OF WAR REPORTING BY MARTHA GELLHORN

THE FIRST HOSPITAL SHIP

June 1944

There were four hundred and twenty-two bunks covered with new blankets, and a bright, clean, well-equipped operating room, never before used. Great cans marked "Whole Blood" stood on the decks. Plasma bottles and supplies of drugs and bales of bandages were stored in handy places. Everything was ready and any moment the big empty hospital ship would be leaving for France.

The ship itself was painfully white. The endless varied ships clotted in this English invasion port were gray or camouflaged and they seemed to have the right idea. We, on the other hand, were all fixed up like a sitting pigeon. Our ship was snowy white with a green line running along the sides below the deck rail, and with many bright new red crosses painted on the hull and painted flat on the boat deck. We were to travel alone, and there was not so much as a pistol on board in the way of armament, and neither the English crew and ship's officers nor the American medical personnel had any notion of what happened to large conspicuous white ships when they appeared at war, though everyone knew the Geneva agreement concerning such ships and everyone wistfully hoped that the Germans would take the said agreement seriously.

There were six nurses aboard. They came from Texas and Michigan and California and Wisconsin, and three weeks ago they were in the U.S.A. completing their training for this overseas assignment. They had been prepared to work on a hospital train, which would mean caring for wounded in sensible, steady railway carriages that move slowly through the green English countryside. Instead of which they found themselves on a ship, and they were about to move across the dark, cold green water of the Channel. This sudden switch in plans was simply part of the day's work and each one, in her own way, got through the grim business of waiting for the unknown to start, as elegantly as she could. It was very elegant indeed, especially if you remembered that no one aboard had ever been on a hospital ship before, so the helpful voice of experience was lacking.

We had pulled out of the harbor in the night, but we crossed by daylight and the morning seemed longer than other mornings. The captain never left the bridge and, all alone and beautifully white, we made our way through a mine-swept lane in the Channel. The only piece of news we had, so far, was that the two hospital ships which preceded us struck mines on their way over, fortunately before they were loaded with wounded soldiers and without serious damage to the personnel aboard. Everyone silently hoped that three would be a lucky number; and we waited very hard; and there was nothing much to see except occasional ships passing at a distance.

Then we saw the coast of France and suddenly we were in the midst of the armada of the invasion. People will be writing about this sight for a hundred years and whoever saw it will never forget it. First it seemed incredible; there could not be so many ships in the world. Then it seemed incredible as a feat of planning; if there were so many ships, what genius it required to get them here, what amazing and unimaginable genius. After the first shock of wonder and admiration, one began to look around and see separate details. There were destroyers and battleships and transports, a floating city of huge vessels anchored before the green cliffs of Normandy. Occasionally you would see a gun flash or perhaps only hear a distant roar, as naval guns fired far over those hills. Small craft beetled around in a curiously jolly way. It looked like a lot of fun to race from shore to ships in snub-nosed boats beating up the spray. It was no fun at all, considering the mines and obstacles that remained in the water, the sunken tanks with only their radio antennae showing above water, the drowned bodies that still floated past. On an LCT near us washing was hung up on a line, and between the loud explosions of mines being detonated on the beach dance music could be heard coming from its radio. Barrage balloons, always looking like comic toy elephants, bounced in the high wind above the massed ships, and invisible planes droned behind the gray ceiling of cloud. Troops were unloading from big ships to heavy cement barges or to light craft, and on the shore, moving up four brown roads that scarred the hillside, our tanks clanked slowly and steadily forward.

Then we stopped noticing the invasion, the ships, the ominous beach, because the first wounded had arrived. An LCT drew alongside our ship, pitching in the waves; a soldier in a steel helmet shouted up to the crew at the aft rail, and a wooden box looking like a lidless coffin was lowered on a pulley, and with the greatest difficulty, bracing themselves against the movement of their boat, the men on the LCT laid a stretcher inside the box. The box was raised to our deck and out of it was lifted a man who was closer to being a boy than a man, dead white and seemingly dying. The first wounded man to be brought to that ship for safety and care was a German prisoner.

Everything happened at once. We had six water ambulances, light motor launches, which swung down from the ship's side and could be raised the same way when full of wounded. They carried six litter cases apiece or as many walking wounded as could be crowded into them. Now they were being lowered, with shouted orders: "That beach over there where they've got two red streamers up." "Just this side of Easy Red." We lay at anchor halfway between those now famous and unhealthy beaches, Easy Red and Dog Red. "Take her in slow." "Those double round things that looked like flat spools are mines." "You won't clear any submerged tanks, so look sharp." "Ready?" "Lower her!"

The captain came down from the bridge to watch this. He was feeling cheerful, and he now remarked, "I got us in all right but God knows how we'll ever get out." He gestured toward the ships that were as thick around us as cars in a parking lot. "Worry about that some other time."

The stretcher-bearers, who were part of the American medical personnel, started on their long back-breaking job. By the end of that trip their hands were padded with blisters and they were practically hospital cases themselves. For the wounded had to be carried from the shore into our own water ambulances or into other craft, raised over the side, and then transported down the winding stairs of this converted pleasure ship to the wards. The ship's crew became volunteer stretcher-bearers instantly. Wounded were pouring in now, hauled up the lidless coffin or swung aboard in the motor ambulances; and finally an LST tied alongside and made itself into a sort of landing jetty, higher than the light craft that ran the wounded to us, but not as high as our deck. So the wounded were lifted by men standing on the LST, who raised the stretchers high above their heads and handed them up to men on our deck, who caught hold of the stretcher handles. It was a fast, terrifying bucket brigade system, but it worked.

Belowstairs all the partitions had been torn out and for three decks the inside of the ship was a vast ward with double tiers of bunks. The routing inside the ship ran marvelously, though four doctors, six nurses and about fourteen medical orderlies were very few people to care for four hundred wounded men. From two o'clock one afternoon until the ship docked in England again the next evening at seven, none of the medical personnel stopped work. And besides plasma and blood transfusions, re-dressing of wounds, examinations, administering of sedatives or opiates or oxygen and all the rest, operations were performed all night long. Only one soldier died on that ship and he had come aboard as a hopeless case.

It will be hard to tell you of the wounded, there were so many of them. There was no time to talk; there was too much else to do. They had to be fed, as most of them had not eaten for two days; shoes and clothing had to be cut off; they wanted water; the nurses and orderlies, working like demons, had to be found and called quickly to a bunk where a man suddenly and desperately needed attention; plasma bottles must be watched; cigarettes had to be lighted and held for those who could not use their hands; it seemed to take hours to pour hot coffee, via the spout of a teapot, into a mouth that just showed through bandages.

But the wounded talked among themselves and as time went on we got to know them, but their faces and their wounds, not their names. They were a magnificent enduring bunch of men. Men smiled who were in such pain that all they really can have wanted to do was turn their heads away and cry, and men made jokes when they needed their strength just to survive. And all of them looked after each other, saying, "Give that boy a drink of water," or "Miss, see that Ranger over there, he's in bad shape, could you go to him?" All through the ship men were asking after other men by name, anxiously, wondering if they were on board and how they were doing.

On A deck in a bunk by the wall lay a very young lieutenant. He had a bad chest wound and his face was white and he lay too still. Suddenly he raised himself on his elbow and looked straight ahead of him, as if he did not know where he was. His eyes were full of horror and he did not speak. Later he spoke. He had been wounded the first day, had lain out in a field and then crawled back to our lines, sniped at by the Germans. He realized now that a German, badly wounded also in the chest, shoulder and legs, lay in the bunk behind him. The gentle-faced boy said very softly, because it was hard to speak, "I'd kill him if I could move." After that he did not speak for a long time; he was given oxygen and later operated on, so that he could breathe. . . .

If anyone had come fresh to that ship in the night, someone un-wounded, not attached to the ship, he would have been appalled. It began to look entirely Black-Hole-of-Calcutta, because it was airless and ill lit. Piles of bloody clothing had been cut off and dumped out of the way in corners; coffee cups and cigarette stubs littered the decks; plasma bottles hung from cords, and all the fearful surgical apparatus for holding broken bones made shadows on the walls. There were wounded who groaned in their sleep or called out and there was the soft steady hum of conversation among the wounded who could not sleep. That is the way it would have looked to anyone seeing it fresh—a ship carrying a load of pain, with everyone waiting for daylight, everyone hoping for the anchor to be raised, everyone longing for England. It was that but it was something else too; it was a safe ship no matter what happened to it. We were together and we counted on each other. We knew that from the British captain to the pink-cheeked little London mess boy every one of the ship's company did his job tirelessly and well. The wounded knew that the doctors and nurses and orderlies belonged to them utterly and would not fail them. And all of us knew that our own wounded were good men and that with their amazing help, their selflessness and self-control, we would get through all right.

The wounded looked much better in the morning. The human machine is the most delicate and rare of all, and it is obviously built to survive, if given half a chance. The ship moved steadily across the Channel and we could feel England coming nearer. Then the coast came into sight and the green of England looked quite different from the way it had looked only two days ago; it looked cooler and clearer and wonderfully safe. The beaches along this coast were only lovely yellow sand. The air of England flowed down through the wards and the wounded seemed to feel it. The sound of their voices brightened and sharpened, and they began making dates with each other for when they would be on convalescent leave in London.

We saw again the great armada of the invasion, waiting or moving out toward France. This vast directed strength seemed more like an act of nature than a thing men alone could manage. The captain shouted down from the bridge, "Look at it! By God, just look at it!"

American ambulance companies were waiting on the pier, the same efficient swift colored troops I had seen working on the piers and landing ramps before we left. On the quay there were conferences of important shore personages and our captain and the chief medical officer; and a few of us, old-timers by now, leaned over the rail and joked about being back in the paper-work department again. Everyone felt happy and you could see it in all their faces. The head nurse, smiling though gray with weariness, said, "We'll do it better next time."

As the first wounded were carried from the ship the chief medical officer, watching them, said, "Made it." That was the great thing. Now they would restock their supplies, clean the ship, cover the beds with fresh blankets, sleep whatever hours they could, and then they would go back to France. But this first trip was done; this much was to the good; they had made it.

NOTES

1. Martha Gellhorn, *The Face of War* (London: Virago Press, 1986), viii.
2. Ibid.
3. Ibid.
4. Ibid.
5. As quoted in Bernice Kert, *The Hemingway Women* (New York: W.W. Norton, 1983), 286.
6. Gellhorn, *The Face of War*, 22.
7. Ibid., 55.
8. Ibid., 73.
9. Ibid., 89.
10. Kert, *Hemingway Women*, 405–406.
11. Ibid., 410.
12. Gellhorn, *The Face of War*, p. 89–90.
13. Ibid., 90.
14. Martha Gellhorn, *The View From the Ground* (New York: Atlantic Monthly Press, 1988), 108.
15. Ibid., 97.

16. Ibid., 88.
17. Ibid., 97.
18. Ibid., 110.
19. Gellhorn, *The Face of War*, xii.
20. Ibid., xix.
21. Ibid.
22. Gellhorn, *The View From the Ground*, 111.

15

Shelley Mydans

"Perhaps I am best known for a six-word cable I sent through U.S. Army censorship during those dismal few weeks right after Pearl Harbor," Shelley Mydans wrote, "when our troops withdrew to Bataan before the Japanese advance." She had reported on the novice troops of the New Mexico National Guard. They had been bombed at Clark Field and were retreating through Manila. Her employer, *Life* magazine, liked the story but requested that "the next one be on Americans on the offensive." News of the debacle taking place in the Philippines had not reached the United States, so Shelley's reply was the first indication that the U.S. Army was in full retreat. She cabled: "Bitterly regret your request unavailable here."[1] Then the Japanese entered Manila and Carl and Shelley Mydans were interned.

Shelley Mydans was born on the Stanford University campus in 1915. Her father, an English professor, had been invited to establish a department of journalism. Shelley showed no interest in the field, and her father didn't encourage it either. He said he didn't want her to be his student. Her interest was in acting. Enrolled as an English major, she spent the majority of her time with a stock company in San Francisco, then moved to New York when she was twenty or twenty-one years old. Because of the depression, she never did find an acting job, but joined a modern dance group instead. The pay was meager, and her father had died by then, so Shelley looked up a student of her father's who was editor of the *Literary Digest*. She became a reporter and worked there for several years before the *Digest* folded. The *Digest* was famous for having run the first poll on the 1936 election; they predicted a landslide for Landon, who eventually got one or two states. Roosevelt won the election.

Just before the *Digest* ceased to publish, a friend of Shelley's sug-

Shelley Mydans. Photo courtesy of Shelley Mydans.

gested she go to see about a job on the new *Life* magazine, which was started in 1936. She went to the Chrysler Building and discovered that the system at *Life* included editors, writers, and researchers; most of the latter were young women who worked with photographers. Mary Fraser (she eventually married Dan Longwell), head of research who later became the managing editor, interviewed her. "What do you know about pictures?" she was asked. Her answer was, "Nothing." "Well," Miss Fraser answered, "I guess that doesn't matter." Shelley became a researcher in the National Affairs Department.

From this new position Shelley became acquainted with the photographers who came and went, and one of them (there were four or five on the original staff) was Carl Mydans. He was an outstanding *Life* photographer and worked from the inception of the magazine in 1936 until it folded in 1967. A good description of those early years of *Life*, when it was such a huge success, is found in Carl's book, *More than Meets the Eye*. Shelley and Carl were married in June of 1938.

When war started in Europe in September of 1939, *Life* decided it would be interesting to have a photo-reporter team there, so Carl and Shelley were the first *Life* team sent to cover the war. As it turned out, they didn't work together very much during the phony war period. They did cover conditions in England, but Karl went to Finland to photograph the Finnish war with Russia, and Shelley stayed in Sweden. "They didn't want to take care of a woman," she recalls. "They kept me busy doing background for a Swedish essay, then sent me back to England to do a story with another photographer on minesweepers." In the meantime, Carl went to do a story on Italy under Mussolini.

Although both Carl and Shelley became accredited war correspondents, the nature of their assignments changed little. "It was the same work I was doing in New York," she explained, "getting the background, making the arrangements, participating in group journalism."

Shelley was sent to do a story on Portugal, the "Balcony of Europe." When the Germans broke through the Maginot Line in June of 1940, Portugal became a center for spies and refugees. Shelley worked with another photographer, and sent back volumes of material to be culled by *Life* writers. Then the Mydans were called to return home. " 'Europe is dying,' they thought back in New York, and they wanted us young people home—against our will," Shelley recalled. She found work in Washington, while Carl did a story on the navy in Pearl Harbor.

Then toward the end of 1940 they were sent to cover the Sino-Japanese war. "That was real drama," Shelley said. By 1940 the Chinese had been pushed back to the far western provinces and the

Japanese controlled at least the central cities, the highways, and the rail routes in all of eastern China. The capital was in Chungking. The Mydans went by boat to Hong Kong, then got a flight with the China National Air Company (which had American planes and American flyers). They landed on a mud bank in the middle of the Yangtze River. Being in Chungking was like going back three centuries, Shelley recalled. "It was very exciting and we just ran around taking pictures and doing stories as fast as we could." Constant air raids took place, but the actual fighting was further up on the Yellow River. The Mydans traveled to that location, but found it wasn't very active. The area, however, intrigued them. "It was extraordinary," Shelley said, "like going into another century." The accommodations were primitive, but they liked the people—"wonderful people." The Mydans reported on how the Chinese were handling the war with Japan.

The next assignment was to do a story on the Burma Road, but *Life* changed that assignment and sent them back to the Yellow River front. Then they did a series on the preparation for war throughout Southeast Asia, since it was clear that the Japanese had their eye on Thailand, Burma, Malaya, and the Philippines. They were in the Philippines when the Japanese attacked, on the same day as Pearl Harbor was hit. Clark Field was demolished, and the Americans in the area were left with a few American National Guard, a few pilots who had no planes to fly, two or three PT boats, and some Philippine scouts. The Japanese couldn't be stopped and came into Manila, where the Mydans were trapped.

The Mydans were interned with other Americans for about eight months. Then they had the opportunity to go on a Japanese troop ship to Shanghai. They went, because they thought they might have a better chance to be freed since they had connections in Shanghai. After about a year in that camp there was an exchange arranged between American civilians and Japanese civilians, and the Mydans returned home in December of 1943. When commenting about their imprisonment, Shelley remarked, "It wasn't so bad. We were young, we were together, and we hadn't lost anything except our cameras. Other people suffered more than we did." They did lose weight on a rice diet in the first camp, but in Shanghai it was more of a "bread and potatoes" fare, so they did better. The Japanese, Shelley remembered, were very decent to the civilian internees, but could be brutal to the captured American soldiers.

Upon their return to the United States, Shelley took a leave of absence to write a novel based on their prison camp experience while

Carl went to   .o cover the war there. Her novel was called *The Open City*. Tl _.n MacArthur returned to Manila and Carl flew there, but because MacArthur wouldn't allow women correspondents, Shelley went to Pearl Harbor and wrote stories from that location. She then moved on to Guam and wrote about the naval base and flight nurses who flew with wounded soldiers back to base hospitals. Shelley recalls that "I was accredited to the navy, but I was not—because I was a woman—allowed to cover action on naval ships or planes and my articles had to be confined to such things as the navy flight nurses and marine base camps."[2]

Admiral Nimitz's headquarters were situated on CinCPac Hill (abbreviation for Commander in Chief Pacific) on Guam, Shelley recalled. Large quonset huts housed administration, censorship (where correspondents worked), and officer billets where male correspondents slept. By some error of requisition, the quonset huts had Simmons mattresses on the beds. However, the three women correspondents were not allowed to have billets in the quonset huts. The order was, "Women may not lie down on CinCPac Hill." So the women were given cots in tents lower down the hill where the marines were quartered. This was thanks to the marine general in command, Henry L. Larsen. The women correspondents slept in the tents in a barbed-wire compound and were driven back and forth by jeep to their work in CinCPac headquarters. The drivers had to be armed because of stray Japanese on the island. Since enlisted men did not carry side arms, Shelley remembered that "officers had to be assigned to this absurd duty."

Shelley was the first woman assigned to CinCPac, before any nurses or Red Cross women were stationed on Guam. "The extreme attention paid to me was disconcerting," she recalled.

When Manila was secured, MacArthur allowed her to come. She was perhaps the first woman correspondent into Manila, and with Carl she did a story on the operation to invade Japan. By now Shelley was accredited with the army once again. Then the Japanese surrendered, and while the men went to cover the important surrender on the U.S.S. *Missouri*, she was left to write about the surrender of General Yamashita, commander of the Japanese forces on Luzon. She finally got to Tokyo in the fall of 1945, shortly after the surrender. From there she and Carl wrote about the defeated Japanese and the first American troops.

"My work as a war correspondent in World War II," Shelley explained, "was primarily as a writer/researcher for *Life* which meant that much of the time I was working with photographers, making arrangements for their pictures, and writing the background and captions for their stories which were all excerpted and rewritten in New York. It was not a very glamorous job, though I did write signed pieces for *Life* once in a while and send dispatches to *Time* when there was no *Time* correspondent in the field."[3]

The Mydans went briefly to Shanghai after the war was over, and at that point Shelley got a cable asking if she would come home and take over the *Time* radio broadcast. *Time* had a program called the "March of Time" on the ABC network. Shelley wrote and did broadcasting for "Time for Women," a news program. Then, because she was pregnant, she had to decide whether to make a career of being a radio personality or be a mother. She resigned and when the baby was five months old (MacArthur wouldn't let infants under five months into Tokyo), she joined Carl in Japan. He was *Time* bureau chief there, and Shelley worked as a correspondent for two years. She then resigned when her second child was born.

The Korean War started and Carl went back to doing photography, while Shelley moved to California and lived on the edge of the Stanford campus. Later they moved to England together. At present Carl still works for *Time* and the Mydans live in Larchmont, New York.

NOTES

1. Shelley Mydans, letter to author, 13 October 1986.
2. Ibid.
3. Ibid.

16

Mary Welsh

"Sudden, unexpected death is nothing new to American soldiers by now . . ." began the broadcast.[1] This was Mary Welsh's last report related to World War II, a report on how the average G.I. in Europe would react to the death of President Roosevelt. After this final story written for the "March of Time" on April 21, 1945, Mary Welsh left the world of journalism, went to Cuba, and eventually became the fourth Mrs. Hemingway.

Mary Welsh was born in 1908, to parents who were largely self-educated and not wealthy. Her father was a logger and operated a Mississippi riverboat. Her mother was a Christian Scientist. Mary was an only child, born and raised in small towns of Minnesota. Her interest in journalism began early, when the local newspaper editor and his wife came to her house for dinner when she was only a child. After a year at the local state college, she went to Northwestern University to study journalism and support herself with part-time jobs.

After two years of study, she decided to work for a magazine, *The American Florist*. As she wrote, "It was a job and paycheck in a wasteland of unemployment and breadlines."[2] She moved on to a firm that published five weekly "throwaways," neighborhood newspapers given away free. She felt this was a step closer to the newspaper world. Finally, she got a chance to join the *Chicago Daily News*. Although she wanted to cover major stories, such as city hall or crime, she acquiesced to write the women's pages under Miss Leola Allard—not an easy boss to work for! Mary wrote that Miss Allard "taught us how to work and something of how to write. Especially she taught us fortitude."[3]

In 1936 Mary traveled to England, Ireland, and France, and upon her return tried to get an assignment at one of the *Daily New*'s foreign bureaus. Her argument was that there would be a war and that she should be in Europe getting background knowledge. Nothing worked, and she didn't receive a foreign assignment. She then became acquainted with Lord Beaverbrook, who owned some London newspapers. He had invited her to New York and subsequently to tour the Nile with him, but she declined the latter offer. Nevertheless, he told her that if she came to London, he would try to help her find work. Mary went, and got a job with the London *Daily Express*. The editorial floor reminded her more of the throwaway newspaper offices than the *Chicago Daily News*, but she received interesting assignments that made up for the lack of atmosphere.

One of her stories was written in the Netherlands about the birth of Princess Juliana's first child. Another was from Munich in September of 1938, reporting the meeting between Neville Chamberlain and Adolf Hitler. She also wrote from the Czech border about the invasion of the German army. M.L. Stein reports that she was the first female correspondent with the British forces.[4]

Then England declared war on Germany, and Mary managed to go to France and report on the British Expeditionary Force. Finally, on the way back to England she decided, as she put it, "for reasons murky around their edges, that I must stop working for a British newspaper and switch to something American."[5] She resigned from the *Daily Express* and on July 10, 1940, began reporting for the London bureau of *Time*, *Life*, and *Fortune*.

Just a few days after she was hired, Mary began reporting on the German Luftwaffe attacks on London. At the same time she began broadcasting for the BBC; her stories were to be straight reporting about conditions in London. The Blitz attracted much of her attention. "Mary remembers the winter of 1940–1941 as one of terror and destruction. Every night the bombers came and the fires raced from rooftop to rooftop. In the morning as she walked to work she passed the plain gray vans being loaded with dead bodies."[6] These scenes made a deep impression on her, but she decided any emotional reaction would delay her work. She wrote a short piece for *Time*, but they didn't publish it—too grim, was the reason.

Mary had a no-nonsense attitude, was resilient, and could cope with what the war brought. Described as small and shapely, her hair a curly honey-brown, her voice soft and musical, Mary could easily charm others. These feminine features, however, didn't keep her from venturing to London's East End and similar areas especially devastated by the Blitz, and reporting on both the living and the dead. She wrote of an encounter with a little boy four or five years old whose mother had been buried in the rubble—a common occurrence. After reassuring him as best she could, she headed for her office, "to be a mediocre worker that day."[7]

Mary continued to report on the war, and in December 1941 she was sent back to New York, to the *Time* foreign desk. Here she discovered that men were the writers and women the researchers. When one of her stories appeared with her byline, the men avoided her and the women resented her, so it was with relief that she returned to London—not without difficulty, however. Mrs. Helen Shipley, well known to all reporters as the person who headed the State Department's passport division and, according to widespread opinion, made life difficult for them, held up Mary's passport for one reason or another. Mary wrote that she "was no more responsive than an amoeba to *Time*'s requests for my clearance to England."[8]

Finally back in London in 1942, she found herself dismayed by the destruction and danger, which she had rationalized while in New York as being sensationalized because of the distance. She later wrote that the new bombing of London made her nervous. "To get killed and miss the chance of observing history, not only military victory but also what political and economic triumphs might accompany it, or to be mangled into uselessness seemed more than unusually unwelcome that spring."[9]

By 1944 she could write in her diary that she was getting fine compliments from New York for her work. She persuaded her boss to send her to Paris and she covered the first day of the liberation. She also happened to write the only signed article in *Life*'s edition of the week of D-Day. It was about how the U.S. Army handled casualties during the invasion. While reporting from Normandy, she had her driver stop sometimes "so that I could look at abandoned battlefields with their broken and discarded objects. . . . It was bizarre emptiness overhung by a miasma of desolation."[10] When reporting from France and the battalion aid stations, she wrote, "Walking between the long rows of beds in the rear evacuation hospitals, I was struck by their terrible anonymity. Name, serial number, blood type, army unit."[11] She felt that nothing indicated what these men had been before they took part in the Normandy invasion, and nobody cared.

Mary had met Ernest Hemingway in London, and spent time with him in Paris and France. By now estranged from her husband, Noel Monks, a reporter from Australia, she began seeing Ernest more frequently. Although she continued to cover the war from her base in Paris, she also began to admit that "Ernest was becoming more important to her than her job and that a career of wifehood was what she really wanted."[12] On February 27, 1945, she asked for permission from the army to go home. One of the last stories she wrote before her return to the United States was about the work of the Nazi underground forces. This was a sardonic report about the condition of the average German, whom she contrasted with the bony and malnourished people in France. She was appalled at the obvious lack of guilt the German people seemed to feel—she called them a people without conscience.

Mary visited her parents in Chicago, then flew to Havana to begin a life with Ernest Hemingway. They were married in 1946. She continued to write as a free-lancer, but her life centered around Ernest. After his death she wrote her autobiography, *How It Was*. Mary died on November 26, 1986.

NOTES

1. Mary Welsh Hemingway, *How It Was* (New York: Alfred A. Knopf, 1976), 151.

2. Ibid., 29.

3. Ibid., 31.

4. M.L. Stein, *Under Fire: The Story of American War Correspondents* (New York: Julian Messner, 1968), 226.

5. Hemingway, *How It Was*, 53.

6. Bernice Kert, *The Hemingway Women* (New York: W.W. Norton, 1983), 401.

7. Hemingway, *How It Was*, 66.

8. Ibid., 81.

9. Ibid., 92.

10. Ibid., 104.

11. Ibid., 105.

12. Kert, *Hemingway Women*, 413.

17

Virginia Lee Warren

"I didn't appreciate the experience at all at that time. It's looking back on it that I realize that it was one of the great adventures of my life." Virginia Lee Warren, wife of Milton Bracker, recalled her feelings about being a war correspondent for the *New York Times* during World War II. "At the time I just took it for granted. I really wasn't terribly keen to go over—I went mostly because I wanted to go over to be with my husband."

Virginia Lee Warren was born in Winchester, Virginia, on June 14, 1907. Because her mother didn't like the schools in the little towns where the family lived, she had Virginia educated privately, mostly in music and art. Virginia did not receive a college degree.

She got her first job on a small newspaper in Redlands, California, and was women's page editor there. After three years of experience she moved on to the *Washington Post*. "That was very wonderful, of course," she said, "quite a big jump from a little paper like the one in Redlands to the *Washington Post*." She began as fashion editor and did feature stories in women's news. Her major goal, however, was to be in the newsroom. "I finally got there. I was told at the time that I was the first female ever to get in there." She worked at the *Washington Post* for three years and then she met a man from the *New York Times*. "We saw each other six times and got married. I came up to New York and then I stopped working," she stated.

Virginia was happy to be keeping house and doing a little free-lance writing. Then World War II started. Milton Bracker was sent to Europe as a war correspondent. "Everybody, of course, wanted to do something in the war effort," Virginia recalled. "I didn't want to go into an airplane factory—I didn't think I'd be much good at that. I'd probably mess up the machinery. So I got a job on *Time* magazine." Some of her male colleagues from the *Washington Post* had joined *Time* magazine, and they helped her get a job as a writer. "The whole purpose of that," she explained, "was to get me overseas to be with my husband, as a correspondent."

The Office of War Information sent many people overseas, and Virginia could have found a way to Europe by joining that organization, but she wanted to stay in journalism. The *Time* magazine, however, didn't seem interested in sending her to Europe, even though she kept requesting a transfer.

By that time Milton had gone from London to Algiers and other places in Africa, then on to Sicily, Naples, and finally Rome. Virginia asked *Time* magazine if they would send her to Rome, but they responded that they already had all the correspondents they needed in Rome and Italy. "So send me to Cairo," Virginia pleaded. "At least we can visit back and forth once in a while." Virginia added later, "I was pretty naïve about the war!" That request wasn't granted either.

Milton came home on leave after the Brackers had been separated for eighteen months. He talked to the editors of the *New York Times* and pointed out that Virginia had had experience on the *Post* and on *Time* magazine. Personnel from the *New York Times* called the *Washington Post* and asked for a reference. "Send her," replied the editor of the *Washington Post*. "She is very conscientious, a hard worker, and she can do it."

So the Brackers started to put that plan into place, but it wasn't as easy as Virginia thought. First she had to get a special passport. "I'm proud of the one I have kept from that time of a war correspondent," she said. She then sailed on the troop ship. Friends from *Time* magazine said, "For heaven's sakes, the submarine menace is at its worst. Get on a plane and fly!" Virginia could have gone that route, but she wanted to sail, and it turned out to be one of the loveliest voyages she would make.

On the troop ship were about eight thousand men and twelve women—all nurses except for Virginia. The men were all from the air force and she recalls that they played cards all day long. The weather was beautiful, and they would sit on deck (literally, since no chairs were provided) and enjoy the refreshing time.

Virginia arrived in Rome in February 1945 and began covering the Mediterranean theater of operations (MTO). The first day she arrived her husband handed her an assignment, and she worked by candlelight.

They were billeted in the finest hotel in Rome, the Grand. Nobody under the rank of full colonel stayed there, and the Brackers were the only correspondents. "But you know the *Times* carries great weight—everywhere," Virginia stated. She had her own jeep (with a driver) in which to get around the area.

While Milton went to the front and reported, Virginia stayed in Rome because Allied headquarters was there. She wrote under her maiden name, Virginia Lee Warren, and her dispatches did not say Rome, just "Allied Headquarters." She ventured to Florence and several other Italian cities a few times, but received her information from briefings in the press room. Her stories were frequently on the front page—Allied Headquarters stories usually received prominent billing—while Milton's were on the inside pages. "He was up there risking his life, going through all kinds of hardships, and his stories would be inside!" Virginia recalled. "But that was the system at the *Times*."

Another of Virginia's assignments was to cover the Vatican. "The Vatican was hard to get news from," Virginia felt. "Every time I pressed them for information they would say, 'Oh, but we are a church, we don't give that out.' Then when I went at them from a church angle, they would say, 'But we're a government.' They kept me right between—just like having dual citizenship!" Virginia learned of a system that she felt was reprehensible; other reporters who had been there for years would pay a tipster, an old monsignor. Virginia, with the counsel of Milton, refused, and finally an American monsignor began helping her; eventually the other reporters stopped paying the tipster.

Virginia took life as it came. "I worked too hard to know if it was exciting or not. We were on call night and day and never had a day off." At first they lived on the top floor of the hotel, but then were moved to the second. They had a fireplace there and her chauffeur brought firewood for her. "I never suffered any real hardship—never!" She missed the hot water, and the elevators weren't running, but she could buy things at the PX that she couldn't afford at home. "Suddenly I was living on Elizabeth Arden toiletries because they were so cheap there—they were all practically donated by Elizabeth Arden!" Celebrities came by, but Virginia recalled, "We weren't interested in them. That wasn't what we were there for. We didn't think anybody was more interesting than the *New York Times*, naturally."

Virginia often found herself as the only woman around. For example, when the Brackers returned to the United States on a Liberty ship she was the only female on board, and was allotted the shower during lunch time, when the men weren't there. When she went to Florence on a weapons carrier, the troops stopped halfway to eat and go to the restroom—"the latrine, in other words." The line was about half a mile long and she was the only woman; the rest were soldiers.

The suffering of the troops as well as the Italians bothered Virginia. Once she watched some young soldiers come by who had seen some of the fiercest fighting in the north and had lost the battle. They had returned to the city for a day or two, then would go back to fight again. "My heart just ached for them because it would probably be the end of them."

Virginia had not desired to write about the war; she wanted to be with her husband. "The war was pretty close to where I was working. When you're in a place like Rome, you hardly knew what was going on in the other fields."

After the war ended the Brackers visited Switzerland and St. Moritz. Then they were assigned to Mexico in the fall of 1945. She had offered to resign; she told the *Times* editors, "You sent me over to be with Milton because I couldn't come by myself. After the war I can travel with him, and don't need the *Times* to arrange things or get transportation." She did stay with the *Times*, and they spent thirteen months in Mexico. After that they were assigned to Argentina for four years. Virginia did the bulk of the reporting from Argentina because much of the time Milton was traveling throughout South America, reporting from the other countries. When they returned to New York, she quit the paper.

18

Lael Laird Wertenbaker

"Would love to talk about those years!" was Lael Wertenbaker's reply to a letter requesting an interview. "Everything I did was accidental, including the events that led up to my work as a war correspondent."

Lael Tucker was born in Pennsylvania in 1909—by accident, so to speak, she explained, because she was of Southern heritage. She went to school in nine states. As she explained, "My father was a clergyman and very peripatetic, so the truth is I have no education at all. I didn't graduate from anything." Educationally speaking, Lael skipped from grammar school to high school, then to college without graduating. "Educationally speaking I now have two doctorates, but when I have to fill out a page about my education, it is a little embarrassing."

Lael went to work at seventeen in a bookshop, then moved to New York where she worked for the Theatre Guild for a few years. Her plan was to become a playwright. During one weekend she went with a friend of hers to the home of the managing editor of *Fortune*. In the course of an idle conversation, he said to her, "You should work for *Fortune*." Five months later he called and asked her to do some research about show business. "I did a rather spectacular job of research," Lael recalls, and six months later she became a researcher for *Fortune*. This job, as Lael points out, was again an accidental happening, since that had not been in her plan at all.

While at *Fortune* she met Steve Laird who was a Washington reporter for *Time*. After they married they moved to Washington, where she substituted for others who wrote for *Life*, *Time*, and *Fortune*. Then in 1940 *Time* wanted to send the Lairds to Berlin. "It was sort of the 'thing' about teams at that point," she remembered. Lael was to write mostly for *Life*.

They applied for their passports, but the famed Mrs. Shipley would not allow Lael to go to Europe through Lisbon—too dangerous, she said. "As far as I could find out later," Lael recalled, "the only danger in Lisbon was the taxi drivers, and they still are!" Lael explained, "She was trying to keep women out of the European theater." Mrs. Shipley was a powerful woman in the U.S. government, nicknamed "the passport dragon."

Lael then asked, "Can I go the other way," and was lucky enough to hear a "Yes." The Lairds went through Japan, Korea, occupied Manchuria, across Russia on the TransSiberia, through occupied Poland, and into Berlin. The journey took ten weeks, including a quarantine in Siberia because of the bubonic plague in Chungking and Manchuria. They finally arrived in Berlin in the fall of 1940. "It was an extraordinary period, before the U.S. was in the war," Lael said. Times were peaceful for Americans and they were not harassed, largely because of America's nonintervention attitudes. In June of 1941, however, the situation changed and the Lairds left Berlin on the next-to-the-last train. While in Germany Lael had written mostly feature and human interest stories.

The Lairds went home briefly and then returned to London, again as a team. There Lael met Mary Welsh, the only other woman war correspondent. "She didn't like my coming," recalled Lael, but eventually Lael "got very fond of her. She was courageous and a good reporter, if a little inventive."

While in London the Lairds parted ways, and Lael returned to New York in 1942 with Charles Wertenbaker, bureau chief for Time-Life. After they were married, Wertenbaker wanted to return to the war. Harry Luce didn't want him to leave, so Charles threatened to go as an officer if he was not sent to be in charge of war coverage. Lael joined him in London in 1944.

One of Lael's favorite stories from London was related to the subway stations and the people who lived in the underground. When the people were to be moved from one station to another, they experienced a sense of being uprooted. "It was really heartrending." They had been bombed out, or couldn't get into the shelters. "It is the terribly human ones [stories] I remember most tenderly," Lael said.

Lael also recalled going to Dover on the coast, which was being shelled as well as bombed. Children were to be evacuated to the north, but to them being bombed was preferable to being among strange children. "It was very touching. Being sent elsewhere was a nightmare for them."

The Wertenbakers then went to Paris at liberation time. Lael continued to work as a war correspondent. She recalled that both in London and Paris "we were so welcome. You got to know people in a way that I don't think has ever been possible before or since. People treated us like one of them." After the war, Charles handled postwar coverage for Time-Life. In 1947 the Wertenbakers left *Time* and lived in France in the Basque country for some years while they wrote books and did free-lance work.

Charles Wertenbaker died a few years later. Lael stayed on with their two children so that she could provide a transition period for them, and then they returned to the United States. She decided to write for a living instead of taking a regular job so that she could be at home with her children, and subsequently produced fifteen books— six novels, three children's books, and six nonfiction volumes. One of these, *The Death of a Man*, was about Charles's death; this well-known book has been reprinted.

19

Other Women Who Achieved Significance as War Correspondents in World War II

There are more distinguished women war correspondents than one might expect. This chapter enumerates several women who would have merited lengthy chapters of their own in this study, but unfortunately not enough information was found; neither were they personally located. Therefore direct communication was not established.

There were several types of correspondents. This book has not considered the broadcast journalists. Nor has serious discussion been given to those who were specialists in politics and came to the various theaters of war, particularly Europe, in order to write better commentaries. These correspondents served a valuable function as they did a lot of prognosticating about "the cerebral and the celestial side of the war," according to Barney Oldfield, "while the frontline war correspondents were engaged in 'Am I going to live through this day or not?' living on K-rations and not being anywhere near something where you could wash for a period of time. To actually endure the same sort of thing that the so-called G.I., common soldier, would endure."[1]

The women mentioned in this chapter were of the sort who wanted to be in the press camps, with access to the front lines. In almost all cases they wrote for newspapers or wire services; a few who wrote for magazines were included because of the significance of their roles.

Lee Carson was one of the three "Rhine Maidens," along with Ann Stringer and Iris Carpenter. Known as Washington's best-looking woman, she charmed people around her all the way to the front. Accredited with International News Service, Lee arrived two weeks after D-Day. In spite of the army's view that women on the front would distract the soldiers, Lee and the other Rhine Maidens managed to report from the scenes of most action. They asked no favors and took frontline life without complaints.

Lee may have had a beautiful head of red hair and marvelous legs, but when it came to reporting on combat, she was indistinguishable from the rest of her peers as, tired, dirty, hungry, and caked with mud, they banged out stories on their typewriters.

In August of 1944 Lee reported on Liberation Day in Paris, managing to evade the usual army orders. She and two other correspondents arrived in Paris even before the Germans had actually left.

She followed the First Army in its march toward Berlin from Normandy. On the 24th of December in 1944 the battle situation was both critical and fluid. Correspondents complained that no one knew just what territory was whose. Worst of all, they didn't know where the Germans were. That day Jack Frankish with UP, Bill Boni with AP, and Lee were discussing the advisability of going to the front. Jack, who had been part of the trio until then, said, " 'I don't think I'm going out tomorrow unless the picture clears. I've got a wife and a couple of kids. I guess I owe something to them as well as my paper.' 'Okay,' Lee told him. 'That's right, if it's the way you feel. I guess that I'll go out, though. I figure if you got it comin', you get it.' "[2] For the first time in many days, Bill and Lee left Jack behind. When they returned they discovered that Jack had "got it." German planes dive-bombed the press camp in Tongres, leaving no doubt that they thought headquarters was still there. Jack was killed outright.

Lee was an intrepid reporter. One of her colleagues from AP used to complain that he had difficulty getting Lee Carson out of his jeep. "You may think she loves you, but all she wants to know is what the AP's number-one story is that day."[3] Lee, as Barney Oldfield put it, was a well-known habitue of the front line. She returned home after the war, married twice, had a successful career in journalism, and died some twenty years later.

Dixie Tighe was also with International News Service. "International News Service always managed to have some very glamorous reporters," recalls Oldfield.[4] Dixie was the most celebrated of the "sob sisters," as women reporters were labeled who would write stories such as the Lindbergh kidnapping trial and reach women's audiences with an emotional point.

Dixie, according to Iris Carpenter, had a flair for individuality. She even individualized her uniform to the point where it drove military police to a frenzy, and she had a reputation for being able to laugh before breakfast. She was not concerned with some of the mundane problems, such as "little girls' rooms," and handled them in as matter-of-fact way as did most other women on the front.5 When told that if women went to the front additional toilet facilities would have to be provided for them, she and some of her female peers said, "Just issue me a spade and I'll take care of it."

Two other war correspondents who are often named as Dixie Tighe's cohorts were Betty Gaskill and Judy Barden. Betty was accredited with *Liberty* magazine and her husband, Gordon, with *American* magazine. Judy was with the *New York Sun*. She married David Nichols of the *Chicago Sun Times* and now lives in England.

Rita Hume was another INS correspondent. According to Virginia Lee Warren, Rita was very attractive and very daring. She went out on night patrols which was the most dangerous thing to do.

Virginia Cowles covered the Spanish civil war with Martha Gellhorn and traveled frequently to the battle lines. She was a correspondent for the London *Sunday Times*, the *New York Times*, and Hearst newspapers. She covered the Spanish civil war in 1937, reported on the war in Finland in 1940, wrote from England in 1941, and also from Russia, Germany, Czechoslovakia, and Paris. Her experiences in these various theaters of war are chronicled in her book, *Looking for Trouble*.

Virginia was one of very few journalists who witnessed the entry of the German army into Czechoslovakia. She and her colleagues were arrested by the Gestapo, charged with being spies, and sentenced to death. While machine guns were pressed against their stomachs, they managed to argue their way out of being shot.6

Eleanor Packard was born in New York City but spent most of her growing-up years in Washington. She attended the University of Washington and Columbia University School of Journalism. After working three years in advertising, she went to Paris as a reporter for the *New York Herald*. A year later, in Vienna, she married Reynolds Packard of UP. He became the head of the Rome bureau and she was the star reporter. Their reporting took them to Tahiti, China, India, Ethiopia, and Italy.

In 1940 the Italian army had invaded Greece, but reporters weren't allowed to visit the front. Eleanor and Reynolds were worried someone would beat them to the story, so Eleanor doctored up an old pass. The scheme worked and Reynolds got a front-row view of the fighting—in fact, too close because he experienced several harrowing incidents before he finally filed his scoop. He was almost expelled from Italy because of this, but got off with a reprimand. Eleanor and Reynolds wrote the book *Balcony Empire*.

Vanya Oakes graduated from the University of California and went to the Orient in 1932. She stayed there for ten years as a correspondent for United Press, the North American Newspaper Alliance, and the *Christian Science Monitor*. After reporting from much of the Far East, she returned to the United States in late 1941. Her book, *White Man's Folly*, tells about her decade of experiences in the Orient.

Peggy Hull, who had reported on World War I, received her accreditation to cover World War II. In November of 1943 she received her orders and subsequently reported on the war in the Pacific Islands for the North American Newspaper Alliance and the *Cleveland Plain Dealer*. Already in her fifties by the time World War II came around, she wrote compassionately about the G.I.s in the Pacific theater.

Marguerite Higgins is perhaps the most well known among women war correspondents, and much has been written about her already. Although she achieved her fame because of astute reporting during the Korean War, she did go to Europe in August of 1944. She spent most of her time writing from the Paris bureau of the *Herald Tribune*, but did take a jeep trip into Germany when the Nazi government was collapsing. She and a fellow correspondent arrived in Dachau, where the remaining German guards at the prison camp surrendered to them. For this story, Marguerite received the New York Newspaper Women's Club award for best foreign correspondence.

After the official close of World War II, fighting never ended in the Orient and the Pacific. Charlotte Ebener reported throughout these areas as well as Russia for INS. She chronicled her experiences in a book called *No Facilities for Women*.

These women and others who are listed in Appendix A were on the beat, as Oldfield stated, and part of the configuration of realities of the dangers of war experienced by everyone who was where it took place.[7]

At a ball held on February 14, 1941, honoring women war correspondents, Kathleen McLaughlin, president of the New York Newspaper Women's Club, paid tribute to those women on the war fronts. She said, "This reunion of the club members and its friends . . . reflects strongly the tide of the times. It is different from its predecessors, colored over and shot through with the consciousness of stirring events past, present and to come."[8] She lauded the "coterie of women under fire, turning out their daily dispatches as competently as the men beside whom they work." As she read the list of names—Eleanor Packard, Helen Kirkpatrick, Tania Long, Betty Watson, Marie Marlin, Sigrid Schultz, Virginia Cowles, Frances Davis, Anne O'Hare McCormick, Sonia Tomara, Dorothy Thompson, Hazel McDonald—she added that "we . . . envy their assignments and admire their achievements. . . . Here's a 'bravo' for them all. They have done us proud."9

NOTES

1. Colonel Barney Oldfield, interview with author, 11 November 1985.

2. Iris Carpenter, *No Woman's World* (Boston: Houghton Mifflin, 1946), 218–19.

3. Oldfield, interview.

4. Oldfield, interview.

5. Carpenter, *No Woman's World*, 34.

6. M.L. Stein, *Under Fire: The Story of American War Correspondents* (New York: Julian Messner, 1968), 96.

7. Oldfield, interview.

8. "Two News Women Honored For Work," *New York Times*, 15 February 1941.

9. Ibid.

Appendix A: List of Women Reporters for Newspapers During World War II

Atkinson, Oriana T.	*New York Times*
Avery, Marjorie	*Detroit Free Press*
Barden, Judy	*New York Sun*
Bracker, Virginia Lee Warren	*New York Times*
Browne, Barbara	*Christian Science Monitor*
Canenberg, Elsie	North American Newspaper Alliance
Carpenter, Iris N.	London *Daily Herald, Boston Globe*
Cowles, Virginia	North American Newspaper Alliance
Coyne, Catherine	*Boston Herald*
Craig, Elizabeth M.	Gannett Publishing Company
Crost, Lyn	*Honolulu Star-Bulletin*
Daniell, Tania Long	*New York Times*
Deuel, Peggy Hull	*Cleveland Plain Dealer*
Ferber, Edna	North American Newspaper Alliance
Frederick, Pauline	Western Newspaper Union
Glosker, Anita	North American Newspaper Alliance
Hamburger, Edith I.	*Cleveland Press*
Hiett, Helen	Religious News Service
Higgins, Marguerite	*New York Herald Tribune*
Hornaday, Mary	*Christian Science Monitor*
John, Elizabeth B.	*Cleveland News*
Kirkpatrick, Helen	*Chicago Daily News, Sun Times*
Knickerbocker, Agnes G.	*Nashville Tennessean*

Lamport, Sara M.	*New York Post*
Lavelle, Elise	National Catholic News Service
Lloyd, Rhonda	*Philadelphia Evening News*
MacCormac, Isabel	*New York Times*
McCormick, Anne O'Hare	*New York Times*
McLaughlin, Kathleen	*New York Times*
Melendez, Dorothy	*Star Herald*
Meyer, Jane	*Chicago Herald American*
Murdock, Barbara	*Philadelphia Bulletin*
Oakes, Vanya	*Christian Science Monitor*
Phillips, Martha E.	Afro-American Newspapers
Polk, Catherine	*Los Angeles News*
Poor, Peggy	*New York Post*
Prewett, Virginia	*Chicago Sun*
Reston, Sarah J.	*New York Times*
Schultz, Sigrid	*Chicago Tribune*
Skariatina, Irina	*New York Times*
Tomara, Sonia	*New York Herald Tribune*
Whitney, Betsey C.	*Washington Times-Herald*

Appendix B: List of Women Reporters with U.S. Wire Services During World War II

International News Service

Olive Brooks
Lee Carson
Mary M. Diggins
Charlotte Ebener
Rita Hume
Inez Robb
Mary Thayer
Dixie Tighe
Candace Vanderlip

Associated Press

Helen Camp
Ruth B. Cowan
Flora Lewis
Cynthia Lowry
Bonnie Wiley

United Press

Harriet C. Hardesty
Hazel Hartzog
Eleanor C. Packard
Ann Stringer
Vanya Oakes

Appendix C: List of Accredited U.S. Women Journalists During World War II

Atkinson, Oriana T.	*New York Times*
Avery, Marjorie	*Detroit Free Press*
Barden, Judy	*New York Sun*
Beeby, Nellie B.	*American Journal of Nursing*
Bess, Dorothy	*Saturday Evening Post*
Blakeslee, Mrs. Victor	*Collier's*
Bourke-White, Margaret	*Time*
Bracker, Virginia Lee Warren	*New York Times*
Bridgman, Julie	*Liberty*
Brooks, Olive	International News Service
Browne, Barbara	*Christian Science Monitor*
Camp, Helen	Associated Press
Carson, Lee	International News Service
Carpenter, Iris N.	London *Daily Herald*, *Boston Globe*
Chapelle, Georgette M. (Dickey)	*Look*
Cochrane, Jacqueline	*Liberty*
Cookman, Mary C.	*Ladies' Home Journal*
Cowan, Ruth B.	Associated Press
Cowles, Virginia	North American Newspaper Alliance
Coyne, Catherine	*Boston Herald*
Craig, Elizabeth M.	Gannett Publishing Company

Cravens, Kathryn	Mutual Broadcasting System
Crost, Lyn	*Honolulu Star-Bulletin*
Danenberg, Elsie	North American Newspaper Alliance
Daniell, Tania Long	*New York Times*
Davis, Gladys	*Life*
Decormis, Anne McCormick	*Fortune*
Deuel, Peggy Hull	*Cleveland Plain Dealer*
Diggins, Mary M.	International News Service
Disney, Dorothy	*Saturday Evening Post*
Drake, Catherine	*Reader's Digest*
Durdin, Margaret L.	*Time*
Ebener, Charlotte	International News Service
Evans, Druscilla	*New York Post*
Ferber, Edna	North American Newspaper Alliance
Finan, Elizabeth S.	*Harper's Bazaar*
Finch, Barbara M.	Reuters
Flanner, Janet	*New Yorker*
Fleeson, Doris	*Woman's Home Companion*
Frank, June M.	*This Month*
Frederick, Pauline	Western Newspaper Union
Freeman, Beatrice	*Magazine Digest*
Gaskill, Betty	*Liberty*
Gellhorn, Martha	*Collier's, Time*
Gingrich, Helen	*Esquire-Coronet*
Glosker, Anita	North American Newspaper Alliance
Gould, Beatrice B.	*Ladies' Home Journal*
Green, Janet	*Trans-Radio Press*
Hager, Alice R.	*Skyways*
Hamburger, Edith I.	*Cleveland Press*
Hardesty, Harriet C.	United Press
Harmon, Dudley Anne	United Press
Hartzog, Hazel	United Press
Hiett, Helen	Religious News Service
Higgins, Marguerite	*New York Herald Tribune*
Hill, Carol	*Collier's, Redbook*
Hollingworth, Clare	*Time*
Hornaday, Mary	*Christian Science Monitor*
Howard, Rosemary	*Newsweek*
Hume, Rita	International News Service

Jacobs, Ann L.	*Young America*
Jacoby, Annalee	*Time*
John, Elizabeth B.	*Cleveland News*
Kempner, Mary Jane	Condé Nast
Kirkpatrick, Helen	*Chicago Daily News*
Knickerbocker, Agnes G.	*Nashville Tennessean*
Kopf, Dorothy Thompson	Bell Syndicate
Kuhn, Irene	NBC
Lamport, Sara M.	*New York Post*
Landau, Ida B.	Overseas News Agency
Lavelle, Elise	National Catholic News Service
Lecoutre, Martha	Tri-Color
Lewis, Flora	Associated Press
Lloyd, Rhonda	*Philadelphia Evening News*
Lochridge, Mary P.	*Women's Home Companion*
Lowry, Cynthia	Associated Press
Lucas, Lenore	Overseas News Agency
MacCormac, Isabel	*New York Times*
Mann, Erika	*Liberty*
Martin, Cecelia (Jackie)	*Ladies' Home Journal*
McCormick, Anne O'Hare	*New York Times*
McLaughlin, Kathleen	*New York Times*
Melendez, Dorothy	*Star Herald*
Meyer, Jane	*Chicago Herald American*
Meyers, Debs	*Yank*
Miller, Mrs. Lee	Condé Nast
Miller, Lois Mattox	*Reader's Digest*
Moats, Alice L.B.	*Collier's*
Muller, Mary T.	*Reader's Digest*
Murdock, Barbara	*Philadelphia Bulletin*
Mydans, Shelley	Time-Life
O'Brien, Mary H.	Fawcett Publications
Offner, Philippa G.	*Life*
Packard, Eleanor C.	United Press
Palmer, Gretta Clark	*Liberty*
Palmer, Mary B.	*Newsweek*
Parker, Pegge	*American Weekly*
Perkins, Alice K.	Fairchild Publications
Phillips, Martha E.	Afro-American Newspapers

Polk, Catherine	*Los Angeles News*
Poor, Peggy	*New York Post*
Prewett, Virginia	*Chicago Sun*
Pringle, Helena	*Women's Home Companion*
Putnam, Eva B.	Trans-Radio Press
Rappoport, Joan (Ann Hunter)	Western Australia Institute of Technology
Reston, Sarah J.	*New York Times*
Reusswig, Martha S.	*Collier's*
Robb, Inez	International News Service
Robertson, Ruth A.	Press Syndicate
Robinson, Iona	*Saturday Review of Literature*
Rocho, Ethel P.	*Collier's*
Schultz, Sigrid	*Chicago Tribune*
Severyns, Marjorie	*Time*
Skariatina, Irina	*New York Times*
Smith, Beverly	*Collier's*
Stirling, Monica	*Atlantic Monthly*
Stringer, Ann	United Press
Thayer, Mary V.	International News Service
Tighe, Dixie	International News Service
Tomara, Sonia	*New York Herald Tribune*
Vanderlip, Candace	International News Service
Vandivert, Margrethe	*Time*
Wertenbaker, Lael Laire	Time-Life
Whitney, Betsey C.	*Washington Times-Herald*
Wiley, Bonnie	Associated Press
Winkler, Betty	Press Alliance
Winn, Mary Day	*This Week*

Not on accredited list:
Boothe, Clare
Burdette, Leah
Oakes, Vanya
PM
Time-Life
United Press, Press Alliance, *Christian Science Monitor*

Bibliography

"Awards Given by Newspaper Women's Club." *Herald Tribune*, 15 May 1943.

Barry, John. "Iris Carpenter Gets First Glimpse of U.S." *Boston Globe*, 4 June 1945.

Carpenter, Iris. *No Woman's World*. Boston: Houghton Mifflin, 1946.

———. "Globe Writer Recalls 'Her Greatest Thrill.' " *Boston Globe*, 9 December 1948.

Chapman, Art. "Defiant Reporter Got Story." *Fort Worth Star-Telegram*, 21 April 1985.

Collins, Chris. "Star-Bulletin Reporter Brought the War Home." *Honolulu Star-Bulletin*, 1 October 1987.

Collins, Jean E. *She Was There: Stories of Pioneering Women Journalists*. New York: Julian Messner, 1980.

Cowan, Ruth. Associated Press dispatch, 23 June 1944.

———. Associated Press dispatch, 13 July 1944.

———. Associated Press dispatch, 1 January 1945.

Coyne, Catherine. "Americans and Russians Join Forces at the Elbe." *The Boston Herald*, 27 April 1945.

———. "Soldiers More Alike Than Not, Says War Correspondent Coyne," 29 April 1945. Reprinted in *The Cape Codder*, 23 April 1985.

Crost, Lyn. "A Story About Shorty." *Honolulu Star-Bulletin*, n.d.

———. "Daniel K. Inouye Wins DSC in Action in Italy." *Honolulu Star-Bulletin*, 26 October 1945.

———. "Doc Kometani Spells Home to Boys of 100th Regiment." *Honolulu Star-Bulletin*, 19 May 1945.

———. "French Bury Last of 18,000 Jews Slain in Nazi Concentration Camp." *Honolulu Star-Bulletin*, 16 April 1945.

———. "Gen. Clark Strong in Praise of Hawaii Troops of 442nd." *Honolulu Star-Bulletin*, 20 April 1945.

———. "Handling Mules." *Honolulu Star-Bulletin*, n.d.

———. "Islanders at Dachau." *Honolulu Star-Bulletin*, 3 July, 1945.

———. "Islanders Can Take It." *Honolulu Star-Bulletin*, n.d.

———. "Islanders Strum Ukes." *Honolulu Star-Bulletin*, 11 June 1945.

———. "Moving Fast, Taking Town, All in a Day's Work for Hawaii Soldiers." *Honolulu Star-Bulletin*, 20 April 1945.

————. "Patch Names Hawaii Soldiers as 'Among Best in American Army.' " *Honolulu Star-Bulletin*, 19 April 1945.

————. Letter to author, 28 September 1986.

Egelhof, Joseph. "A Celebrated Voice of Experience Speaks Out Against Nazi Dangers." *Chicago Tribune*, 28 November 1977.

Emery, Edwin, and Michael Emery. *The Press and America: An Interpretative History of the Mass Media*. Englewood Cliffs, N.J.: Prentice-Hall, 1978.

Gellhorn, Martha. *The Face of War*. London: Virago Press, 1986.

————. *The View From the Ground*. New York: Atlantic Monthly Press, 1988.

Goodnow, Mrs. John M. "Letters to the Editor." *Boston Globe*, 20 March 1945.

Haywood, A.M. "Letters to the Editor." *Boston Globe*, 20 March 1945.

Hazard, Jack. "Letters to the Editor." *Boston Globe*, 20 March 1945.

Hemingway, Mary Welsh. *How It Was*. New York: Alfred A. Knopf, 1976.

Holt, Carlyle. "Even More Attractive Than Photo, Says Holt." *Boston Globe*, 19 April 1945.

Hudson, Catherine Coyne. Letter to author, 4 April 1987.

"Inez Robb's Column." *Editor and Publisher*, 24 October 1953.

"Inez Robb Wins Award." *New York Times*, 5 February 1948.

Kert, Bernice. *The Hemingway Women*. New York: W.W. Norton, 1983.

Kirkpatrick, Helen. "What the Soldiers Think." *The New Yorker Book of War Pieces*. New York: Reynal and Hitchcock, 1947.

Knightley, Phillip. *The First Casualty*. New York: Harcourt Brace Jovanovich, 1975.

Lewis, Flora. Letter to author, 18 February 1985.

Long, Tania. "Ex-Liner Fights Warship and Saves British Convoy." (clipping).

————. "83 Children are Among 293 Dead as Nazis Torpedo Refugee Liner." *New York Herald Tribune*, 22 September 1940.

————. "R.A.F. Fires Visible for 70 Miles." *New Chronicle* [London], from the *Herald Tribune* Bureau, 13 September 1940.

————. Letter to Lester Markel, 9 July 1944.

————. Letter to author, 11 November 1986.

————. "Where Hitler Lives Like a God." *Herald Tribune*, 6 January 1940 or 1941.

Lyons, Leonard. "Clips from Loose-Leaf Notebook." (Newspaper clipping).

Marzolf, Marion. *Up from the Footnote*. New York: Hastings House, 1977.

McClendon, Sarah. "The Stories of Women Journalists." *The Blade* (Toledo, Ohio), 17 November 1985.

Monbleau, Marcia J. "World War II Link-Up in Germany Forty Years Ago This Week." *The Cape Codder*, 23 April 1985.

Moats, Alice-Leone. *Blind Date With Mars*. Garden City, N.Y.: Doubleday Doran & Co., Inc., 1943.

Moulton, Mrs. Deborah D. "Letters to the Editor." *Boston Globe*, 20 March 1945.

Mydans, Shelley. *The Open City*. Garden City, N.Y.: Doubleday Doran, 1945.

————. Letter to author, 13 October 1986.

"Newspaper Club Cites Reporters." *New York Times*, 15 May 1943.

Oakes, Fanny B. "Letters to the Editor." *Boston Globe*, 28 March 1945.

Oldfield, Colonel Barney. *Never a Shot in Anger*. New York: Duell, Sloan and Pearce, 1956.

————. Interview with author. 11 November 1985.

"Rebirth of France." *New York Times*, 2 September 1944.

"Refugees." *New York Times*, 21 November 1945.

Riess, Curt, ed. *They Were There: The Story of World War II and How It Came About.* New York: G.P. Putnam's Sons, 1944.

Robb, Inez. *Current Biography 1958.*

Ross, Ishbel. *Ladies of the Press.* New York: Harper, 1936. Reprint 1974.

Schilpp, Madelon G., and Sharon M. Murphy. *Great Women of the Press.* Carbondale, Ill.: Southern Illinois University Press, 1983.

Schultz, Sigrid. Autobiographical notes from the *Tribune* archives. Chicago, Ill.

Schultz, Sigrid. "Hitler Gazes at Stars to Guide His Decisions." *Chicago Tribune,* 13 July 1939.

———. "Crossing Europe to Peace! A View by Miss Schultz." *Chicago Tribune,* 1 March 1941.

Shelton, Isabelle. "Takes Off for Europe at the Drop of a Hat." *Washington Star,* 7 August 1952.

"Sigrid Schultz, 87, Hitler's Enemy." *Overseas Press Club Bulletin,* 1 June 1980.

"Sigrid Schultz is Dead; Early Berlin Correspondent." *Chicago Tribune,* 16 May 1980.

"Sigrid Schultz Sees Blitz—or a 3 Year War." *Chicago Tribune,* 5 March 1941.

Sperber, A.M. *Murrow: His Life and Times.* New York: Freundlich Books, 1986.

Stein, M.L. *Under Fire: The Story of American War Correspondents.* New York: Julian Messner, 1968.

Stringer, Ann. "The Enemy Has Been Cut in Two: Texan Found Herself at the Front Lines of History." *Fort Worth Star-Telegram,* 21 April 1985.

———. "Frau Himmler Maintains She is Still Proud of Her Husband." United Press release.

———. "Mrs. Mussolini Weepingly Recalls Her Happy Early Days with Dead Dictator." United Press release.

———. "Torgau Meeting With Russians is Both Gay and Strenuous." United Press release.

———. "Yanks Dash Ahead in Race for Rhine." United Press release.

"Supermen in a Dither." *New York Times,* 19 October 1944.

"Task of Occupation Declared in Peril," *New York Times,* 23 November 194?.

Thomas, Helen. Letter to Ruth Cowan, 19 January 1987.

Tomara, Sonia. "On the Roads of France." *The New Yorker Book of War Pieces.* New York: Reynal and Hitchcock, 1947.

"Tribune Writer Says Red Pact Tickles Berlin." *Chicago Tribune,* 25 August 1939.

"Two News Women Honored For Work." *New York Times,* 15 February 1941.

"U.S. Occupation Fails to Break Nazis' Grip." *New York Times,* 25 April 1946.

Webster, Mrs. J.J.F. "Letters to the Editor." *Boston Globe,* 20 March 1945.

Wiley, Bonnie. "First AP Woman Correspondent in the Pacific Relives Past Through Chance Encounter." AP Cleartime (no other publication information available).

———. "Japs Can't Beat Goin' Jessie, John D., Curly." *Seattle Post-Intelligencer,* 30 June 1945.

———. "Pacific Front." Associated Press release (no other publication information available).

———. "Woman Writer in Plane Sees Desperate Battle on Okinawa" (no other publication information available).

———. Letter to author, 19 July 1986.

———. Letter to author, 6 September 1986.

Index

About the Author

LILYA WAGNER is Vice President for Institutional Advancement at Union College in Lincoln, Nebraska; she also teaches courses in journalism and communications. She is the author of *Peer Teaching* (Greenwood Press, 1982).